PHONICS
WORKBOOK
FOR KIDS
MW01628807

Welcome!

This book belongs to:

____

Thank you for choosing our Phonics Workbook! It's great to see that you enjoy doing these activities as much as we do!

This is a big workbook! It was made for you to make sure you get to do all the activities you could ever want. It'll offer hours of entertainment and a refreshing way to both unplug and improve your brain functions through phonics activities, coloring, and more!

A1

ABC Phonics

Aa Aa

Bb Bb

Cc Cc

Dd Dd

Ee Ee

Ff Ff

Gg Gg

Hh Hh

Ii Ii

Jj Jj

Kk Kk

Ll Ll

Mm Mm

Nn Nn

Oo Oo

Pp Pp

Qq Qq

Rr Rr

Ss Ss

Tt Tt

Uu Uu

Vv Vv

Ww Ww

Xx Xx

Yy Yy

Zz Zz

A2

How To Put A Word Together

Let's apply some letters!

Let's look at the word "cast."

Trace the letters!

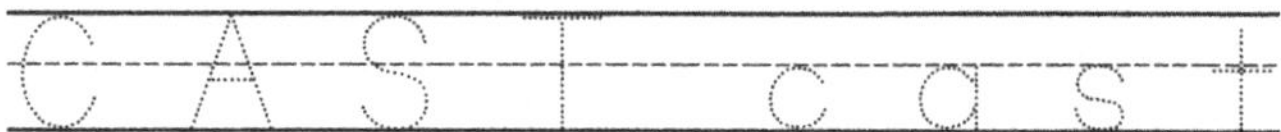

Sound out each of these letters.

With these letters, we can make some other words!
Sound them out:

cat	sat	at	as

Consonants and Vowels

There are two kinds of letters in the alphabet. The letters a, e, i, o, u, and y are vowels. The other letters, b, c, d, f, g, h, j, k, l, m, n, p, q, r, s, t, w, x, y, and z, are consonants. Notice that the letter y can be either one!

When you make a vowel noise, your mouth and vocal chords are wide open! Try saying any of the vowels listed above out loud, and see that your tongue, lips, and teeth don't touch each other. Nothing blocks the air coming out of your throat.

Make some other sounds—like m, b, or l—and notice how you have to move the muscles of your face, lips, tongue and throat to make them come out right!

Go through the words below. Outline or doodle around the consonants in red and around the vowels in blue. Try saying the words out loud as you draw and notice how different sounds are made.

plan	**run**	**east**	**bat**
hop	**long**	**see**	**mom**

Consonants Double Up

Sometimes, a word will have two copies of a consonant right next to each other, like in "ball." Don't worry—it usually doesn't change the sound in English! Some of these words include double consonants; some don't. Circle the correctly spelled word in each row.

Double L	llazy	smille	spill
Double R	carry	hairry	earr
Double S	eassy	fuss	ssame
Double M	comment	mmap	aimm
Double F	ffire	puff	ffit

With these letters, we can make some other words!
Sound them out:

ba___

dre___

si___y

mi___

flu___y

su___er

A5

Complete The Word

Trace the consonant with the right beginning or ending sound!

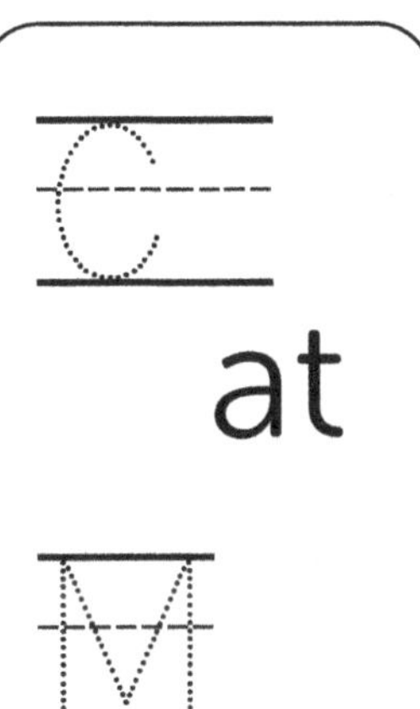

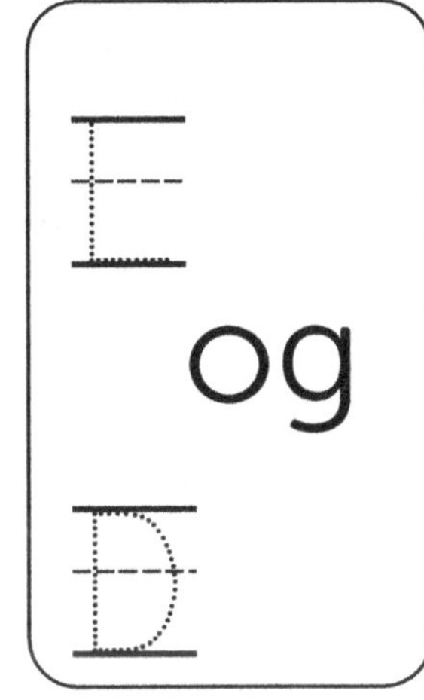

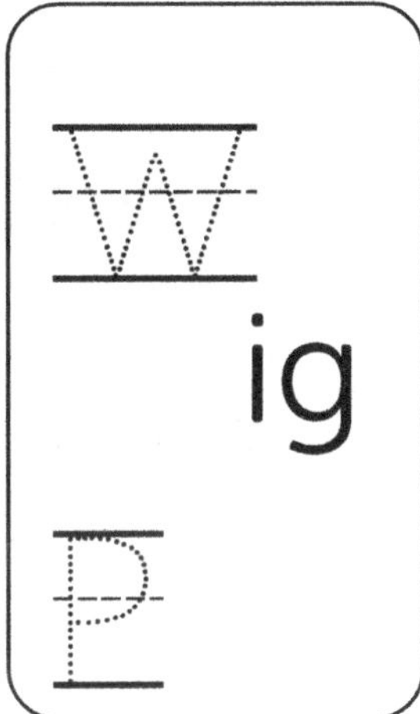

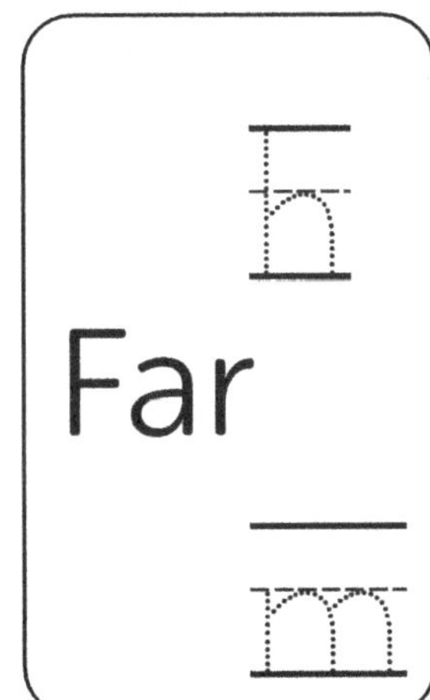

Chaining Daisies

Choose the right flower from the field to start or finish a chain!

H S l J X

B u

a m

F o

a m

p a i

A7

Charm Bracelet

Write in the beginning or ending sound to name the charm!

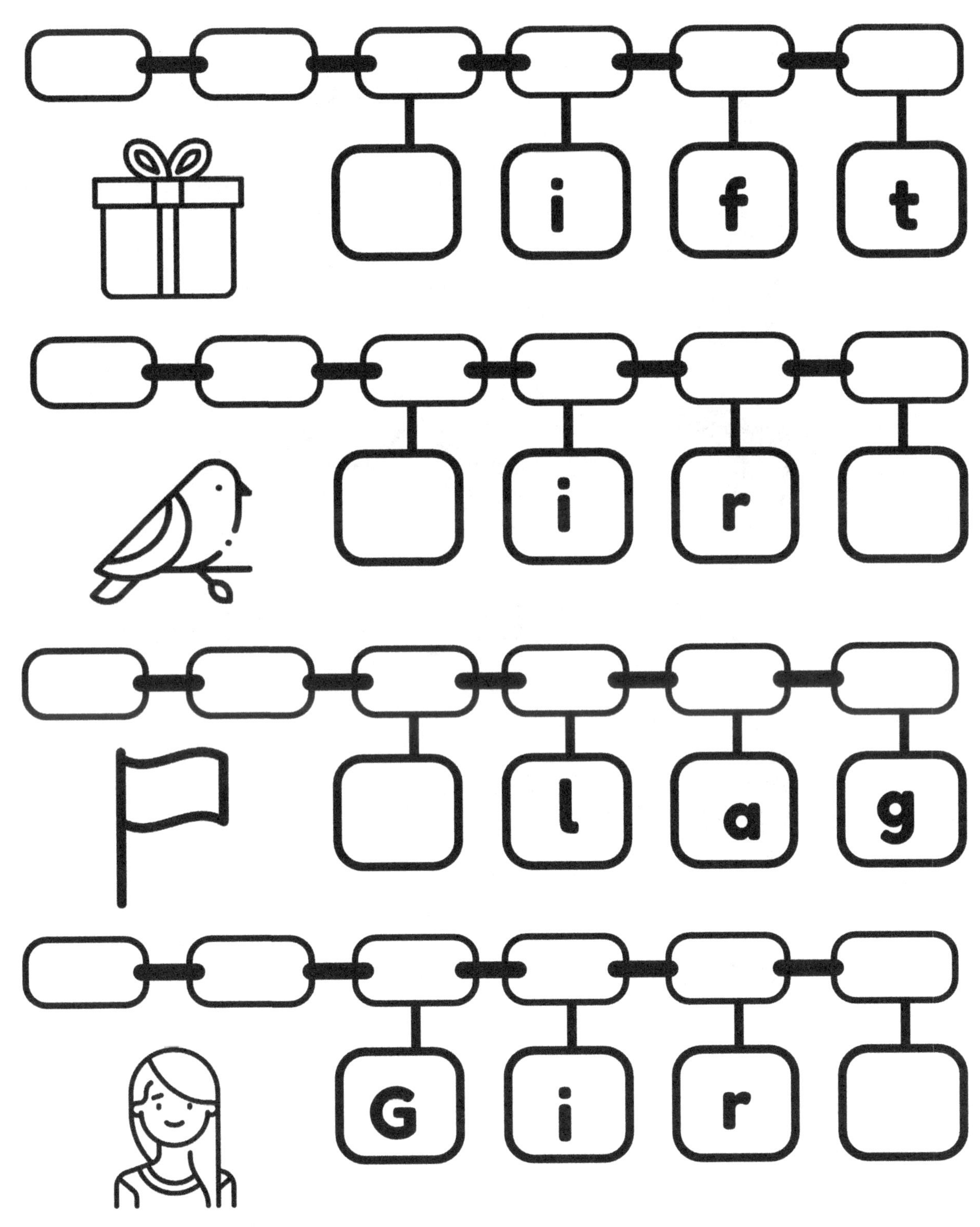

Consonant Fill-in

Use the letters and sounds you've learned to finish naming the pictures.

_ r e e

F _ o w e _

_ o o _ e

U _ b _ e l l a

O _ t o _ u _

_ a i _ b o _

_ a _ e r _ e _ o n

A9

Changing C

The letter c usually makes a hard /k/ song, as in the word "cake." Sometimes, it makes a soft /s/ sound, as in the word "slice."

Read these words aloud and sort them!

cane icy mice cash cent fact

Hard C	Soft C

Do you see a pattern? That's right, c makes a soft /s/ sound when the letter after it is an i, y, or e. In "slice," the letter after c is an e, so it is soft.

Name each of these pictures—is the c hard or soft?

_ _ _

_ _ _ _

_ _ _ _ _ _

G Goes Either Way

Like the letter c, the letter g has two sounds: one hard /g/ sound, as in "grass," and a soft /j/ sound, as in "giraffe." G makes its soft sound if the letter that comes after it is e, i, or y, just like c does!

Soft G = Red　　Hard G = Black

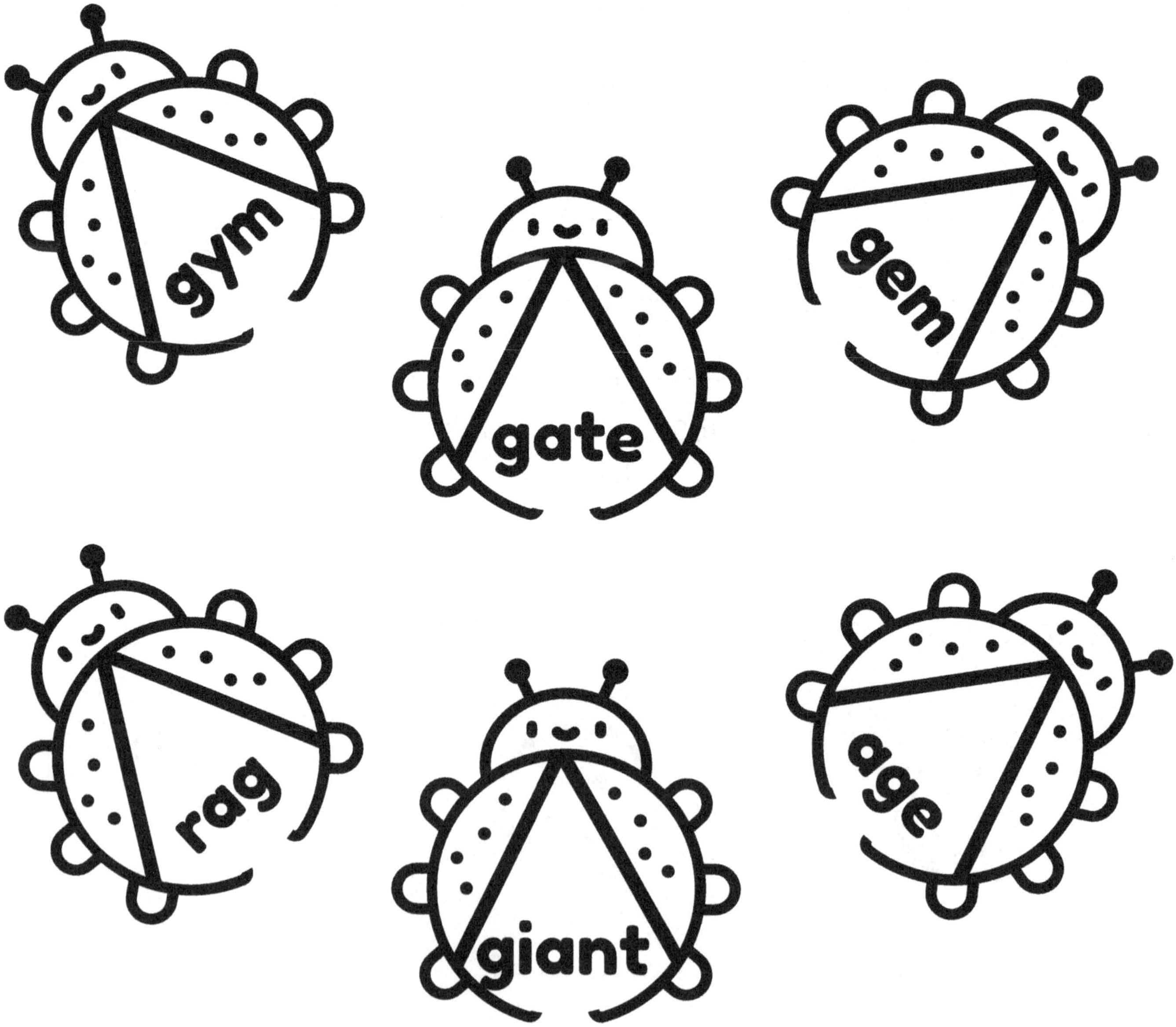

gym

gate

gem

rag

giant

age

A11

Long and Short Vowels

Vowels (A, E, I, O, U) can make more than one sound! Trace some examples:

Short Vowel Sounds	Long Vowel Sounds
Aa Aa Apple	Aa Aa Acorn
Ee Ee Egg	Ee Ee Hero
Ii Ii Whistle	Ii Ii Bike
Oo Oo Frog	Oo Oo Joke
Uu Uu Duck	Uu Uu Glue

Why Is Y Special?

Sometimes, the letter Y is a consonant. Other times, it's a vowel; and it can have two vowel sounds!

yes
vowel or consonant?

bab**y**
vowel or consonant?

law**y**er
vowel or consonant?

yellow
vowel or consonant?

bic**y**cle
vowel or consonant?

happ**y**
vowel or consonant?

monke**y**
vowel or consonant?

year
vowel or consonant?

A13

Y Is A Thief

When Y is a vowel, it can steal the sound of either I or E! Y can be a long e, as in baby, or a long i, as in shy. Sort the words.

rely pretty fly dry windy fry candy puppy apply cycle lazy kitty

Long E Sound	Long I Sound

A14

Color My Vowel

Color the letter that completes the word.
The first one is done for you.

c **o** / e w	b u / a th
m u / o g	w i / o ng
f a / i sh	sh e / o ll
fr a / o g	m a / u p
t u / e lip	b y / u gs

A15

Hop On The Train

Write in the vowel to complete the word!

A16

The Long Or Short Of It

Long A = Red Short A = Orange Long E = Yellow
Short E = Green Long I = Blue Short I = Puple

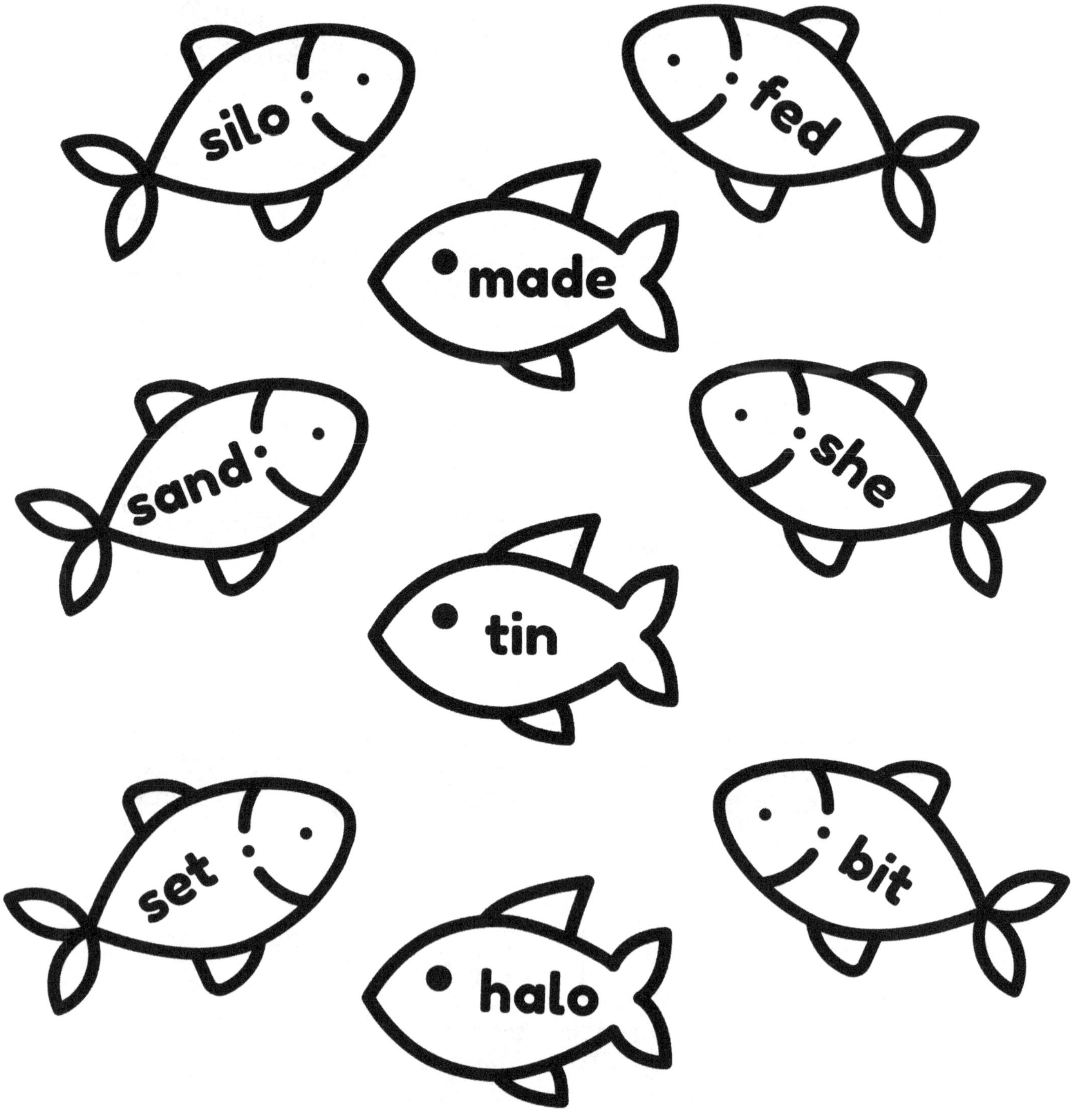

silo
fed
made
sand
she
tin
set
bit
halo

A17

More Vowel Fishing

Long O = Red Short O = Orange Short U = Yellow
Long U = Green Y As E = Blue Y As I = Purple

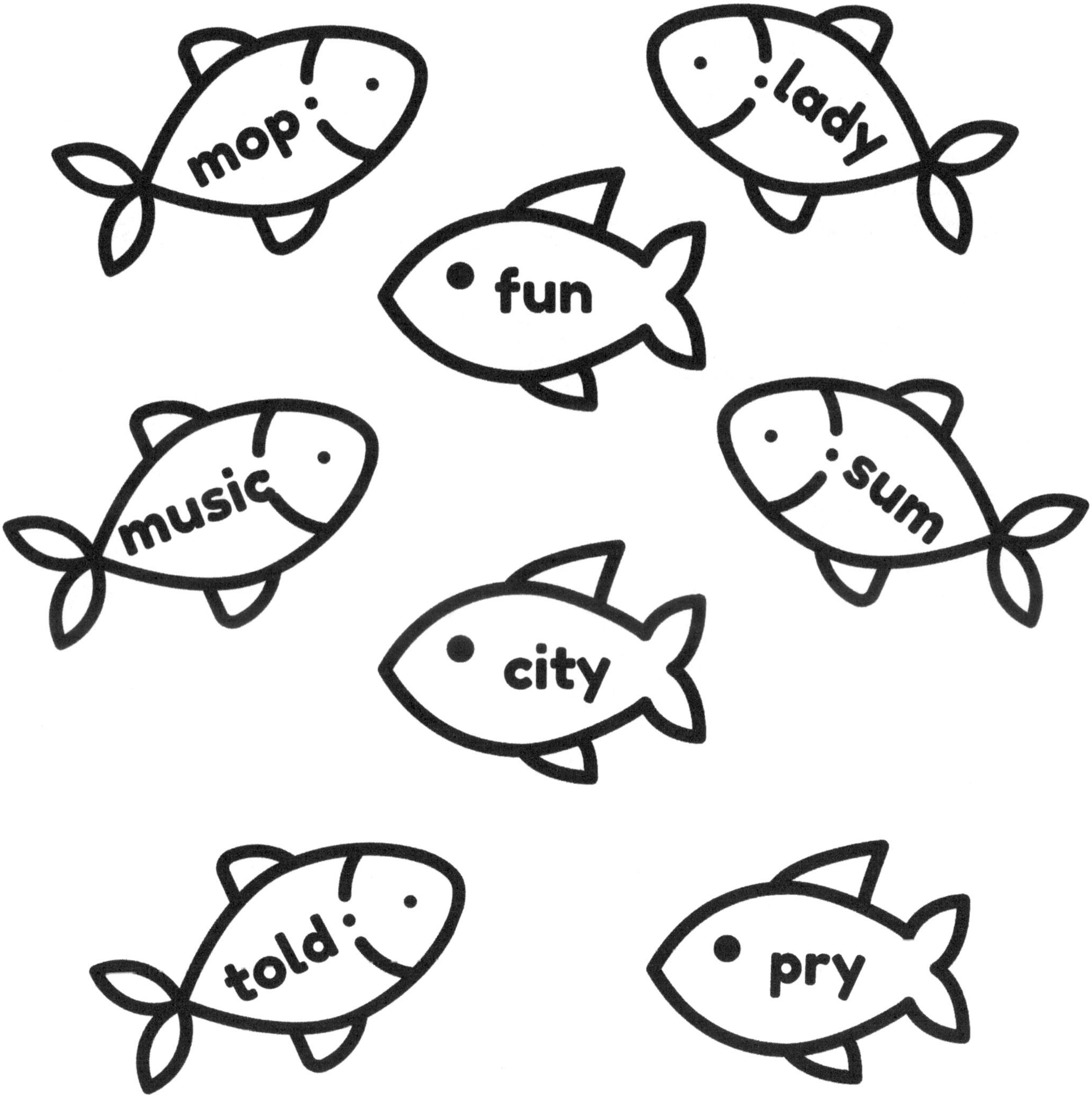
mop
lady
fun
music
sum
city
told
pry

A18

Bossy R

As you've seen, vowels are often affected by the other letters around them. One thing that can change a vowel's sound is a bossy R! When a vowel is followed by the letter r, the vowel makes a new sound.

Read these word pairs aloud and note the difference.

cold / cord	**stamp / star**	**bun / burn**

Circle the words with a bossy r.

make	**ruler**	**purple**	**rain**
alarm	**rope**	**chair**	**puppy**
girl	**leapt**	**sport**	**car**

A19

Missing Bossy R

Fill in the vowel-r cluster to complete each word.

b _ _ d

y _ _ n

st _ _ m

fing _ _

f _ _ k

c _ _ n

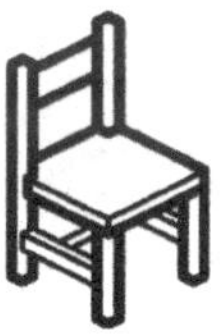

cha _ _

be _ _

p_ _ se

Use Your CVCs

A CVC word goes consonant, vowel, consonant. Write in the CVC that names the picture.

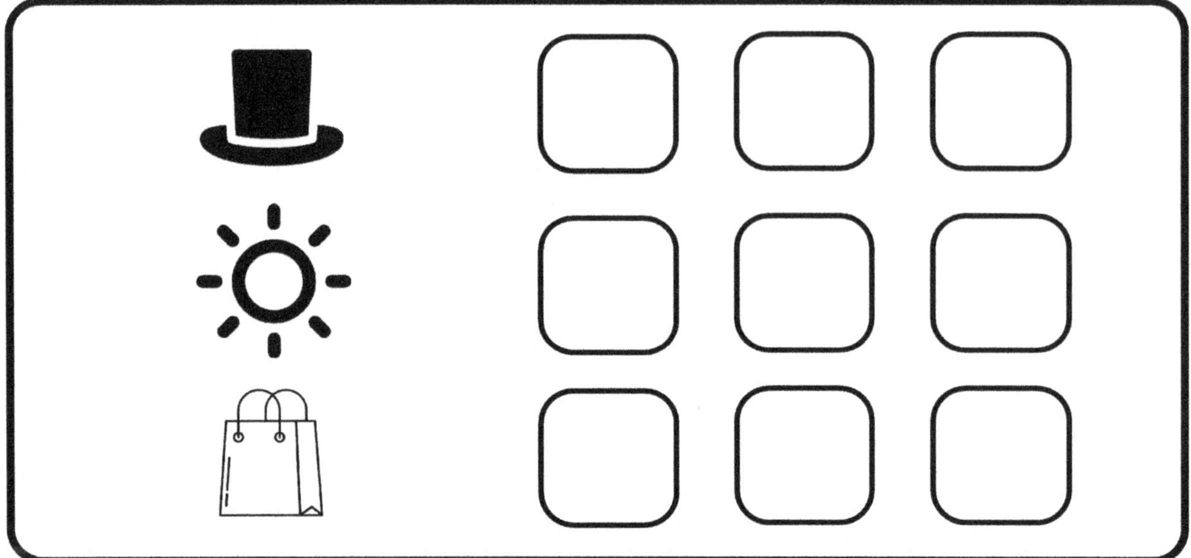

Guess The CVC

Rectangular storage container:

A glass you drink out of:

The number that comes after nine:

Flying mammal that likes caves:

The opposite of lose:

Defining Digraphs

A digraph is a group of multiple letters that work together to make one single sound! The letters can be consonants or vowels. Trace some examples.

Wheel wh	Photo ph	Shell sh	Cheese ch

Path th	Ghost gh	Knight kn	Wing ng

Write wr	Nail ai	Feet ee	Glue ue
		SOAP	
Book oo	Leaf ea	Soap oa	Coins oi

Spot A Digraph

There are two digraphs in chick!

The c and h come together to make one /ch/ sound, while the c and k combine to make a /k/ sound.

Which of these words has a digraph in it? Underline the digraph.

melon	fry	thorn	bad	cave

1	try	sad	met	bath	core
2	cash	man	lid	bun	rods
3	harp	beach	fly	make	bar
4	color	baby	tip	ways	pick

Trigraphs

Sometimes, three letters make one sound. These are a bit harder to use and not as common as digraphs. Say each word out loud, and notice how the trigraph makes just one sound.

Watch tch

Beauty eau

Light igh

Bridge dge

Find the Trigraphs

I sometimes fidget in class.

1. The sun is bright when it is high in the sky.
2. I put my clothes back in the bureau and my food back in the fridge.
3. Today we match, and we look beautiful.

A24

Sh Or Ch?

The digraphs **sh** and **ch** sound similar. For each image, say its name and circle the correct digraph.

sh / ch

sh / ch

sh / ch

Write in **'sh'** or **'ch'** to finish each word!

_ alk

_ell

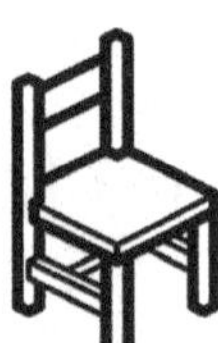

_ air

_ ips

A25

The Two Th Sounds

The digraph **'th'** makes two sounds, one hard and one soft.
See if you can tell them apart!

Hard Th **Sound**	**Soft** Th **Sound**
Mo**th**er	Mo**th**

Sort These Words:

bath **they** **father** **math** **thorn**
this **birthday** **there**

Find The Clusters!

Read these sentences and circle or underline all the digraphs and trigraphs.

On a ship, you can knit warm sweaters, watch for whales, or use a knife to carve wood.

1. My birthday is in a month!

2. I am going to be eight.

3.There will be chocolate ice cream with cherries.

Shooting Stars

Fill in the digraph or trigraph to finish the word.

igh ue sh tch

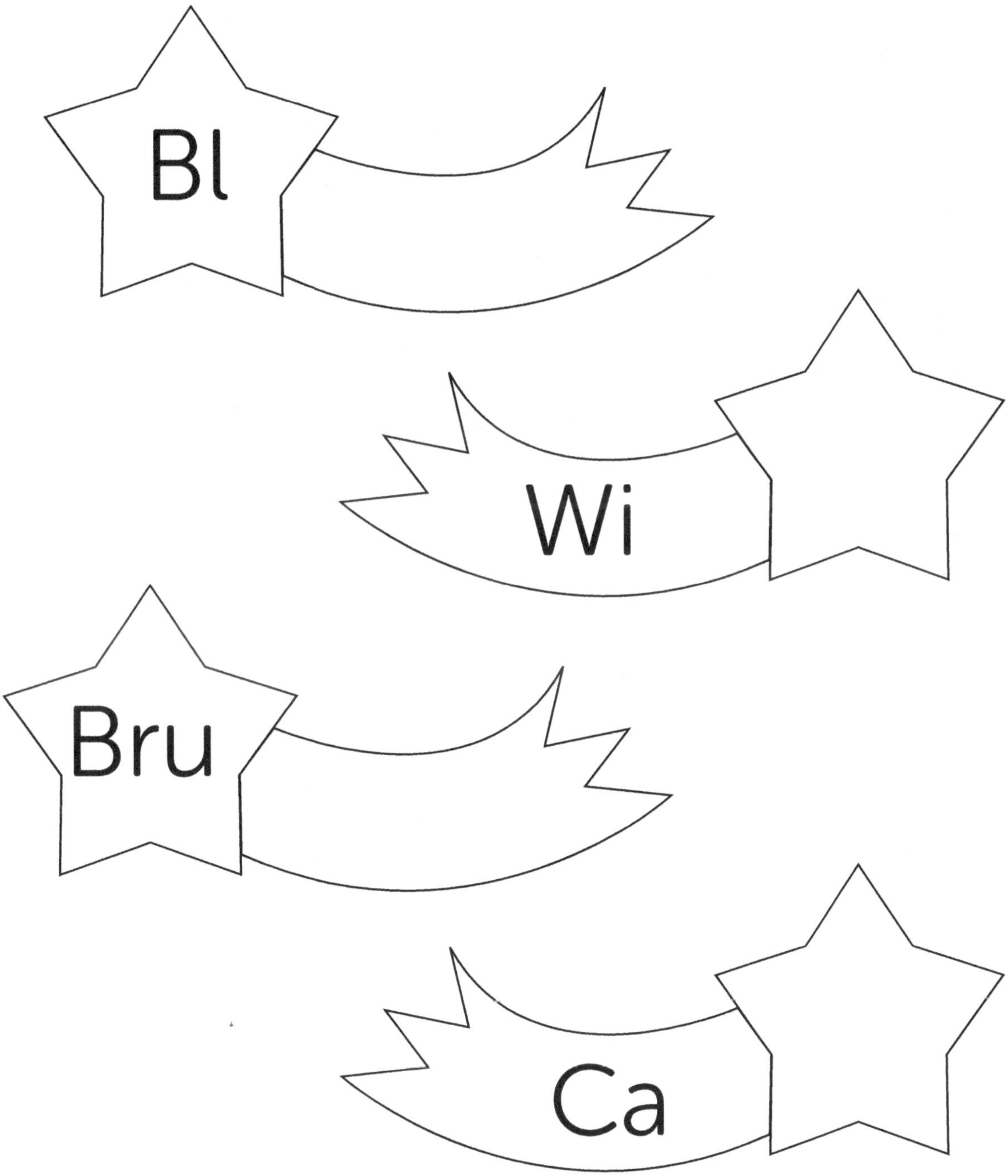

Bl

Wi

Bru

Ca

A28

What Are Consonant Blends?

In a consonant blend, multiple consonants work together to form part of a word.

We've already learned about digraphs, like 'sh' and 'th,' which can bring multiple consonants together to make one sound.

A consonant blend is different because **each letter makes its own sound.**

Read the words below out loud, a few times so you can hear the difference.

In **chew** there are only two sounds, /ch/ and /oo/, because it is made up of digraphs! Repeat the word and see how 'c' and 'h' become 'ch.'

In **flew** there are three sounds, /f/, /l/, and /oo/! 'Ew' is still a digraph, but 'f' and 'l' each make their own sounds. This is how you can tell it is a consonant blend.

Spot The Blends

I can get <u>cl</u>ean.

1. Today I wore a scarf and a shirt with stripes.
2. I love frogs, but not snakes.
3. I like to play! I slide, climb trees, and splash around.

Practicing Consonant Blends

Practice some common blends!

Block bl

Branch br

Clam cl

Crow cr

Dragon dr

Fruit fr

Glitter gl

Grapes gr

Plane pl

Pretzel pr

Slug sl

Smoke sm

Space sp

Stove st

Strong str

Splash spl

A30

A Blend Or A Digraph?

Sound out each word! Now look just at the underlined cluster: does it make one sound, or does each letter in the group make its own sound?

brag
blend or digraph?

chips
blend or digraph?

scrape
blend or digraph?

shave
blend or digraph?

grip
blend or digraph?

thump
blend or digraph?

slide
blend or digraph?

drove
blend or digraph?

when
blend or digraph?

phone
blend or digraph?

twig
blend or digraph?

plate
blend or digraph?

A31

Pick A Balloon

Each of these balloon bunches is missing a consonant blend! Color in the right balloon to finish the word.

Consonant Blend Band-Aids

Oh no! These words are broken. Use the right band-aid to fix them.

Band-aids	Words
sk	☐ unk
sl	wa ☐
fr	☐ ab
gl	☐ eep
cr	u ☐ y
sp	☐ uit

A33

Finish The Word

Fill in the consonant blend.

_ _ ove

_ _ ed

_ _ am

ta _ _ e

_ _ ain

a _ _ee

_ _ ower

_ _ ail

_ _inkle

Defining Diphthongs

Sometimes, two vowels next to each other work together to make a diphthong. A diphthong is just one syllable! It starts with one vowel sound, and moves into another.

Look at the word "boy." The sound made by "oy" starts as a long /o/ sound, but moves into a long /ee/ sound. Say the words "boy" and "join" aloud, and hear the same sound! Those are examples of the same diphthong spelled two different ways, "oy" and "oi."

Read through the examples below aloud, and try to identify which short and long vowels are being voiced in each underlined diphthong, even when spelled differently.

The author wrote a book on law.	
	The cow makes a loud moo.
Now we can go to my house.	

Speaking of moos, the diphthong "oo" can make two different sounds out of the same spelling! Read the sentence aloud and notice the difference between the sounds.

I put my foot into the boot.	

A35

Diphthong Tracing

Fill in the consonant blend.

str<u>aw</u> ____ aw	appl<u>au</u>se ____ au
st<u>ew</u> ____ ew	kaz<u>oo</u> ____ oo
c<u>oi</u>n ____ oi	j<u>oy</u> ____ oy
pl<u>ow</u> ____ ow	cl<u>ou</u>d ____ ou

Find the Diphthongs

Now that you know how to recognize diphthongs, read through these sentences and mark all the ones you can find!

Last August I saw a clown.

I have a toy owl.

I will boil some stew for dinner.

The noise of the fountain is soothing.

I enjoy bowling! My mother taught me how to play.

A37

Broken Hearts

Link the incomplete word to its missing diphthong!

ou	r_m
oo	h_k
aw	s_r
ow	gr_

A38

Build the Word

Write in the diphthong to finish the word!

c			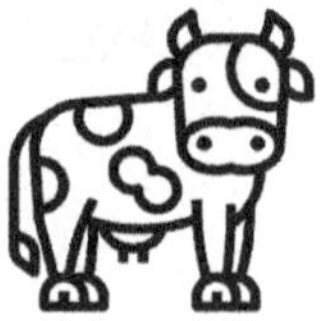
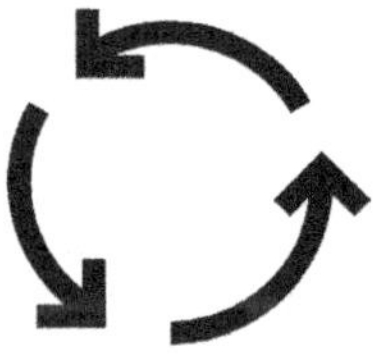	ar		nd
fl		er	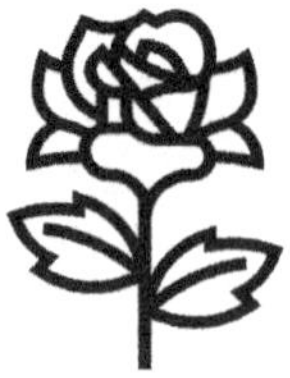
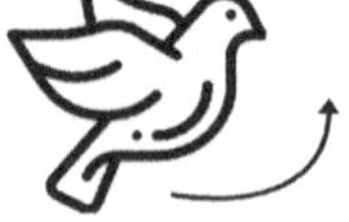	sw		p
cr		l	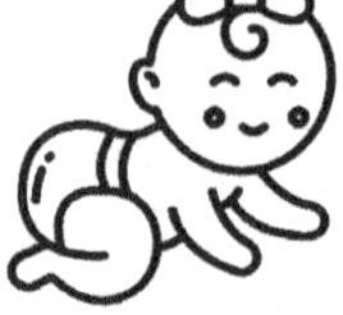

Hello! My name is...

Name each picture with a diphthong word.

___ ___ ___   ___ ___ ___ ___

___ ___ ___ ___   ___ ___ ___ ___

Diphthong Guessing Game

Write in the word (with a diphthong) that answers each clue.

If you're really happy, you might jump for ___ ___ ___!

Someone might say "shhh" if you make too much
___ ___ ___ ___ ___.

Before you swallow food, you have to ___ ___ ___ ___ it.

One way to make art is to ___ ___ ___ ___ a picture with crayons.

How To Put A Word Together

Let's apply some letters!

mall
all

fan
an

jam
am

bang
ang

swing
ing

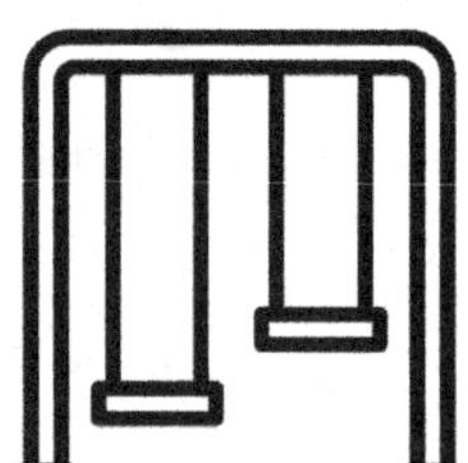

long
ong

lung
ung

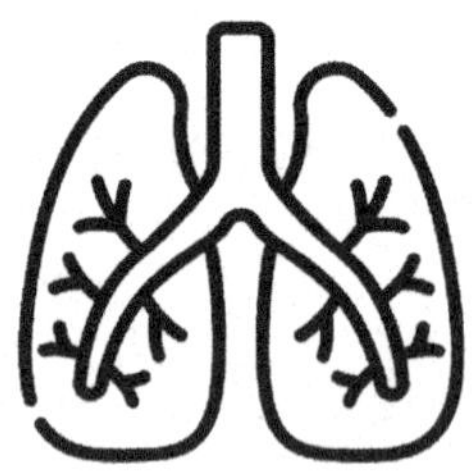

bank
ank

wink
ink

monk
onk

A41

Glued Sounds Color Sort

am = red **an** = blue **ink** = green **unk** = purple

hand	think	sink	stand
trunk	camera	skunk	champ
can	brand	man	wink
fancy	flunk	bunk	lamp
sunk	ham	ramp	land
blink	pink	tan	chunk

Use your colors to write another word for each sound:

am

ink

an

unk

A42

What Is A Prefix?

A prefix is a group of letters that gets added on to the beginning of a word. They change the meaning of the word you add them to, which is called the root word.

Let's look at the verb 'like.'

The opposite of 'like' is 'dislike.'

It contains the whole word 'like,' but it means something totally different! This is because the prefix 'dis' is negative.

Here are some examples of words you might know that have prefixes:

redo	**misbehave**	**unlock**

Notice that if you take the prefix away, you are left with the root word. Take the prefix off of some of these words, and see what you're left with:

reread	**read**
unhappy	
nonstick	
inequality	

A43

Change It Up!

Write each word with the prefix provided and read its new definition.

pre + cooked = ______

Which means: cooked in advance.

pre + judged = ______

Which means: judged in advance.

tri + angle = ______

Which means: three angles.

non + fiction = ______

Which means: not fiction.

over + eat = ______

Which means: eat too much.

A44

All The Nots

Many prefixes mean "not." Underline the parts of these words that act as negative prefixes!

irregular

Means "not regular." When you take away the prefix, you get "regular!"

unusual	**impossible**	**injustice**
nonsense	**misunderstand**	**unhappy**
mistake	**nonfiction**	**informal**

Rewrite all of the prefixes you've found:

A45

Reread It

Re- is a prefix that means "again," and sometimes means "over and over." Add re- to each root word to fit the definition

To wind again. **rewind**

To play again.

To do again.

To search over and over.

To tie again.

To tell again.

What are some other things you can do over and over again? Try coming up with verbs and adding re- to the beginning. Is it a word you've heard before?

A46

What Is A Suffix?

A suffix is a group of letters that gets added on to the end of a word. They change the meaning of the root word, just like a prefix.

Let's look at the verb 'fox.'

If you have more than one fox, that's 'foxes.'

It contains the word 'fox,' but it means something new! This is because the suffix 'es' makes something plural (more than one).

Here are some examples of words you might know that have suffixes:

jumping **louder** **played**

Notice that if you take the suffix away, you are left with the root word. Take the suffix off of some of these words, and see what you're left with:

helpful **help**

slowly ________

bravest ________

sizeable ________

A47

New Words!

Write each word with the suffix provided and read its new definition.

box + es = ____________

Which means: more than one box.

cold + est = ____________

Which means: the most cold.

point + ed = ____________

Which means: pointing in the past tense.

fear + less = ____________

Which means: without fear.

meaning + ful = ____________

Which means: full of meaning.

A48

I Am Learn-ing!

One very common verb suffix is -ing. It changes a verb's tense. If we have the root verb "to learn," we can do it right now in the present by saying "We are learning!" We can also turn the verb into a noun—that's called a gerund—and say "We love learning!"

Connect each verb to its -ing form

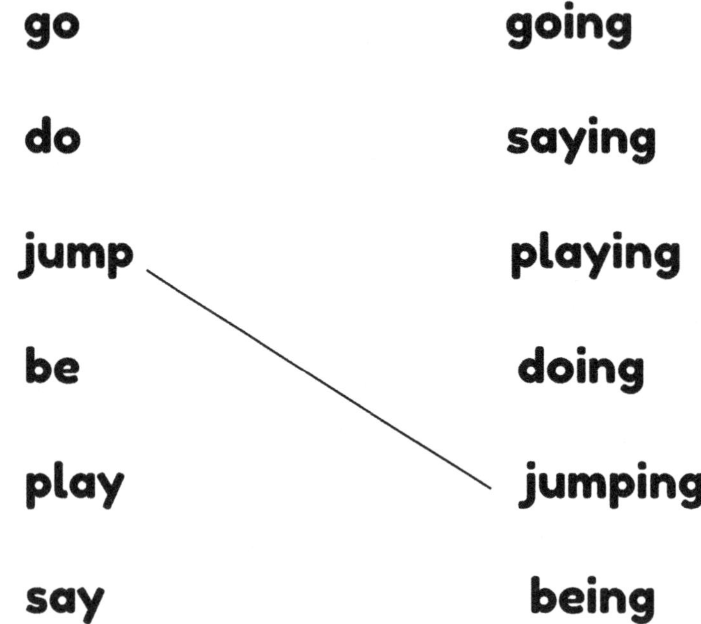

Add -ing to the end of these verbs and rewrite them.

buy	**buying**	**fly**	
help		**see**	
eat		**rain**	

A49

The Two -er Suffixes

-er is a suffix that gets added to the end of words! Sometimes, it means "more!" Cold becomes colder; which means more cold. Old becomes older; which means more old.

-er can also be used as a suffix that means "a person who." Bake becomes baker; which means a person who bakes. Sing becomes singer; which means a person who sings.

Sort the words below into columns; look to the root words for clues about whether they refer to a person or are comparative.

driver weirder tastier rider easier writer
flashier player sleeper happier

A Person Who	More

A50 Comparative Suffixes Are The Best

You know how to use -er when it means "more," but there's another comparative suffix, -est! -est means "most." Something colder is more cold, but if something is the coldest, it's the most cold.

Circle the biggest fish:

When you compare two things, you can use -er. If you compare three or more, you should use -est. Decide which adjective to fill into the sentences below!

My friend is the strongest (strong, stronger, strongest) wrestler on the team.

1. I think my dog is ______ (cute, cuter, cutest) than yours.

2. Macey is the ______ (smart, smarter, smartest) person in my class.

3. My mom is so ______ (nice, nicer, nicest)

4. I am tall! You are even ______. (tall, taller, tallest)

A51

A Prefix Or A Suffix?

Choose whether each word contains a prefix or a suffix.

lawyer prefix or suffix?	predestine prefix or suffix?
trees prefix or suffix?	nicest prefix or suffix?
singer prefix or suffix?	untold prefix or suffix?
lightest prefix or suffix?	untrue prefix or suffix?

A52

Plurals

There are lots of different suffixes to show that there are more than one of a certain thing. Connect the plural noun to the right picture.

fox**es**

pen**s**

cherr**ies**

monkey**s**

lea**ves**

Give it a try! Compare these words to the words above and guess the ending.

loaf ⟶ ____

candy ⟶ ____

box ⟶ ____

glen ⟶ ____

Numeric Ordering

Some prefixes and suffixes indicate an amount! There are many prefixes for each number, but let's learn a few examples.

tricycle	unicycle	bicycle
tri- means: 3	uni- means:_	bi- means:_

septagon	octagon	pentagon
sept- means:_	oct- means:_	pent- means:_

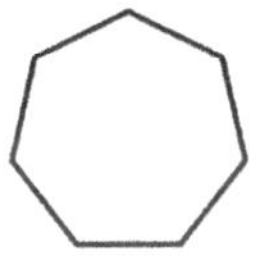

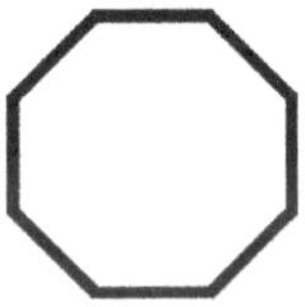

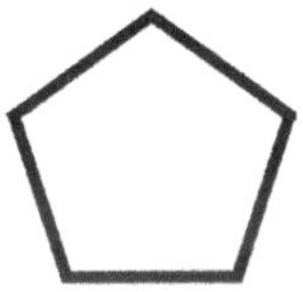

triad	quartet	quintet
tri- means:_	quar- means_	quin- means _

Ends And Beginnings

Find as many prefixes and suffixes as you can.

I dislike your dog. She is smaller than my dog, but much louder.

1. I am reading a nonfiction book about bicycles!

2. Prehistoric dinosaurs are the coolest; I am learning about them in school.

3. The flowering trees in these photos I am reviewing are beautiful! I am happiest out in nature.

4. I am unhappy because I dislike being graded down for misspelling words.

A55

The Silent E

Some words have a silent letter 'e' in them! The 'e' isn't pronounced, but it often changes the pronunciation and meaning of the rest of the word.

The words on the left are all CVCs—they're made up of a consonant, a vowel, and another consonant. Try adding a silent 'e' to the end of each and reading the new word it creates.

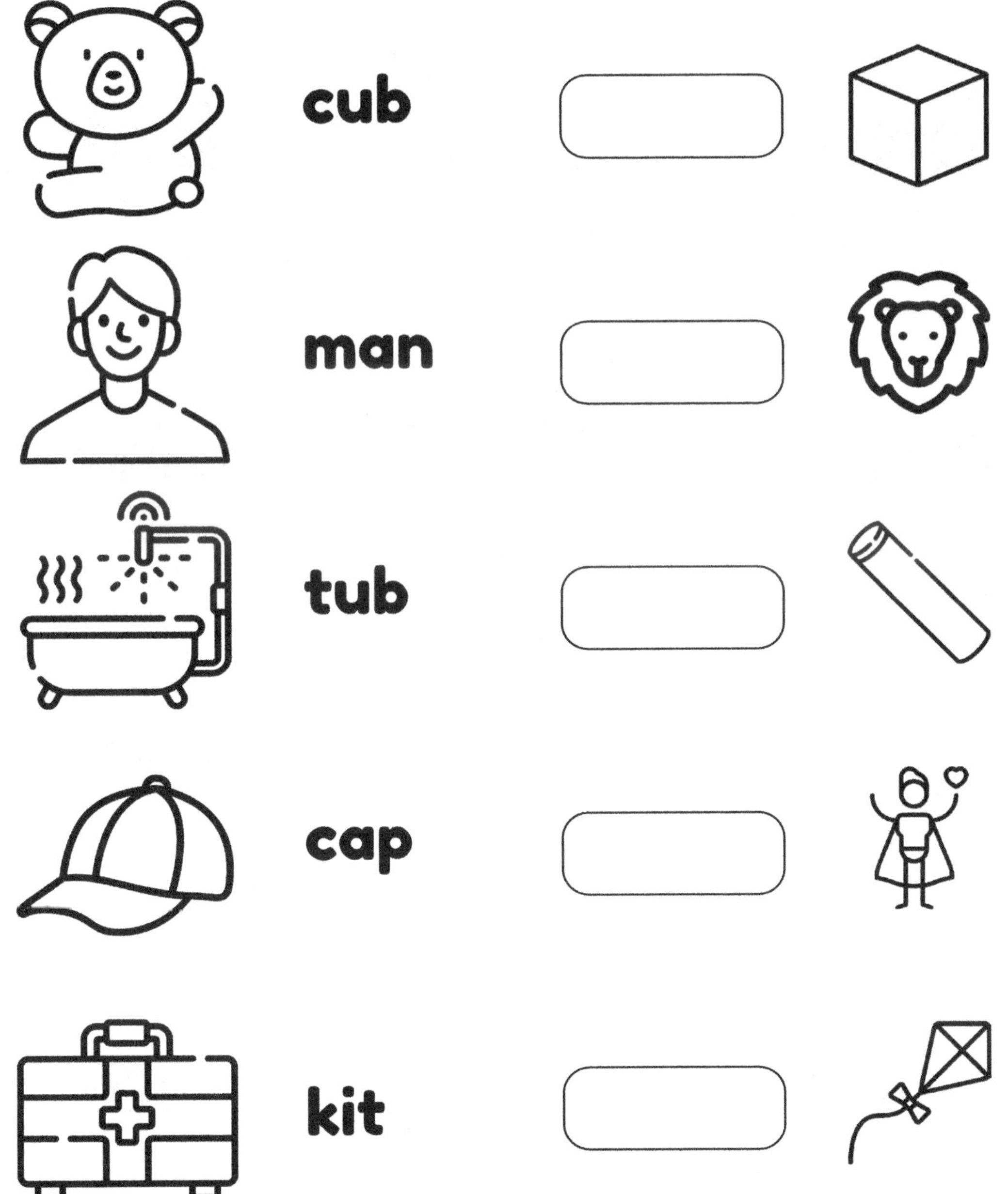

Is There A Silent E?

Circle the correct spelling.

cake  cak

bate  bat

mape  map

take  tak

mare  mar

A57

Does It Need A Silent E?

Decide if each word needs a silent e at the end. If it does, rewrite the word.

bit bite

yes or no?

bug ______

yes or no?

cut ______

yes or no?

div ______

yes or no?

cat ______

yes or no?

rose ______

yes or no?

pan ______

yes or no?

leg ______

yes or no?

A58

Where Do They Belong?

Complete the sentences with silent e words.

face love cute nose nice

1. My baby sister is super ________.

2. I try to be ________ to her.

3. She has a little button ________.

4. It sits in the middle of her ________.

5. I ________ my baby sister.

Magic E

The silent e has lots of uses. Sometimes, it tells the vowel that comes before it in a word to go from a short vowel to a long one. We call this the magic e!

Each of these words has a silent magic e. Take the e away, read the new word, and see how the vowel is shortened!

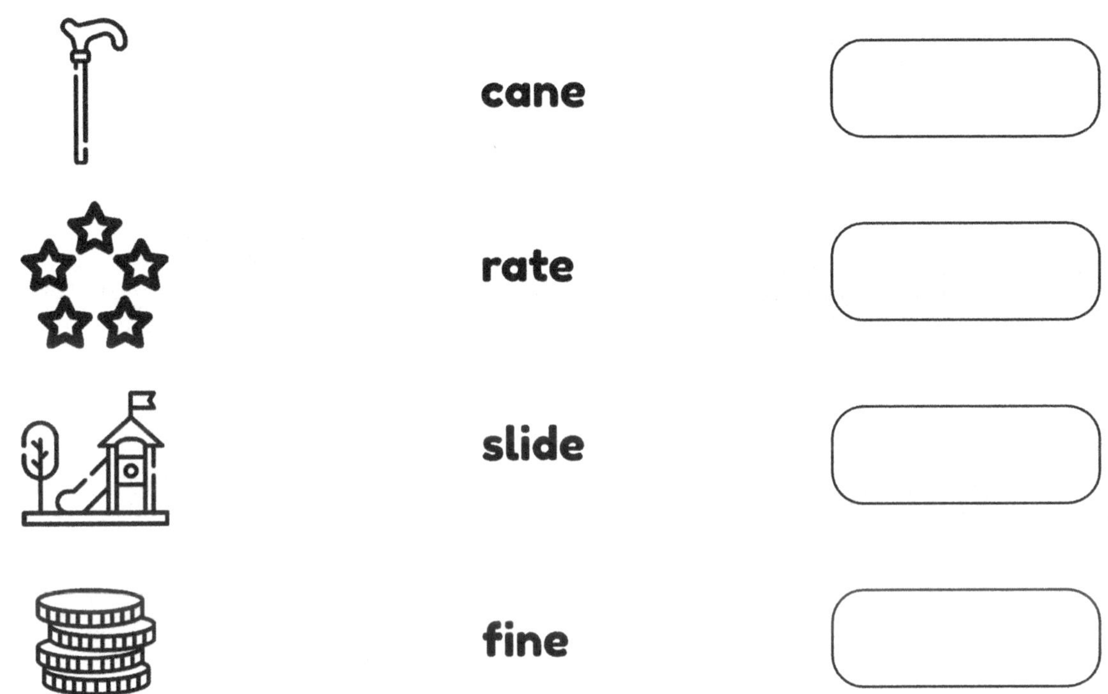

Sometimes, magic e even works when the end of the word is not a vowel followed by a consonant! Here are some examples.

Add a magic e to the end of be, and it becomes

Add a magic e to the end of to, and it becomes

Add a magic e to the end of do, and it becomes

Melting C and G

As we learned earlier, c usually makes the hard /k/ sound, as in "panic." G usually makes the hard /g/ sound, as in "long." When you add a silent e after them, c makes the soft /s/ sound, and g makes the soft /j/ sound.

Match these softened c and g-ending words to the right pictures!

stage	
choice	
large	
once	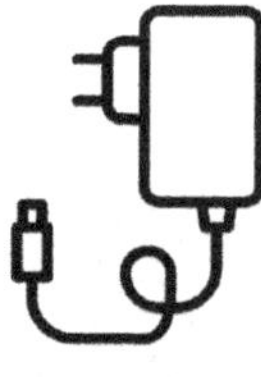
price	
charge	

A61

Phonological Awareness

Read each word below and separate out the sounds. Write the sounds on the lines below.

s h u t	b i b	s o o t
_ _ _	_ _ _	_ _ _
p r y	c h i p	k i t e
_ _ _	_ _ _ _	_ _ _
s a t	t h u m b	p i t
_ _ _	_ _ _	_ _ _
b e d	l i m b	r o p e
_ _ _	_ _ _	_ _ _

A62

Patchwords

All these words are missing their vowels, including some examples of a silent e! Fill the letters in to fix the words.

		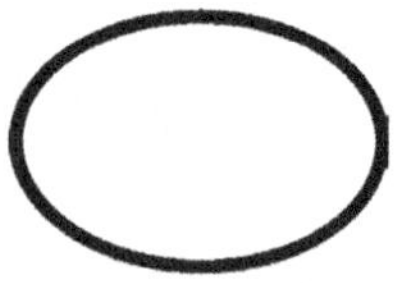
hate	pl _ t _	_v_l

sh _ n e	t _ st _	l _ c _

b _ k _	_ w_ k _	w _ v _

Give Me A Name

Write in the silent e word that names each picture.

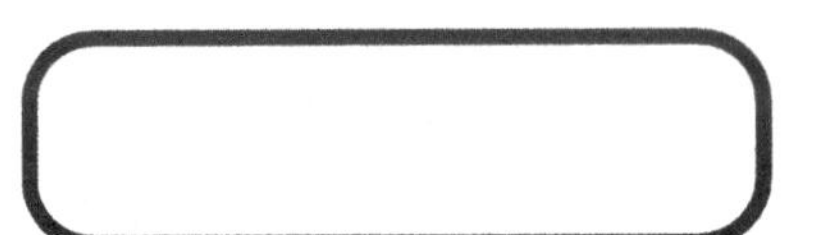

A64

Shhh! Silent Letters

Sometimes, consonants in a word stay silent, just like a silent e. Read these words aloud and circle any letters you can see and not hear.

knit	write	sign
honor	crumb	knight

Read through these sentences and note the words that have silent letters.

I have a **g**nome in my **h**erb garden.

The wreath on my door has bright red berries.

I know that Mary had a little lamb.

The watch on my wrist says it will be eight in an hour.

Silent Letter Match

Match the words with silent letters to their pictures! Circle or underline the silent letter in each word.

crumb 

sword 

ghost 

scissors 

knot 

sign 

A66

Silent Letter Challenge

Based on a similar word with a silent letter, can you decide where the silent consonant goes in each word? Write it in.
The first one is done for you.

chaos	a n cho r	
limb	c l i m	
wreck	r i s t	
knock	n o b	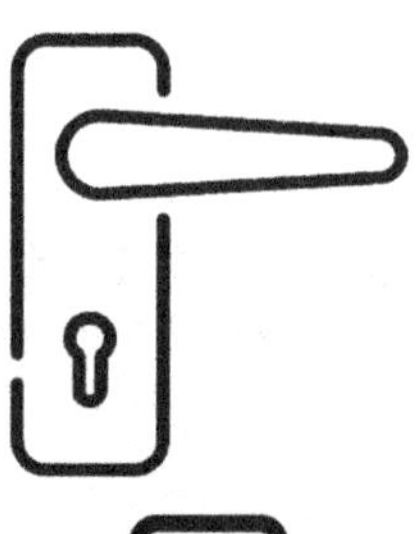
scene	s i e n c e	
wrath	r a p	

What Is Rhyming?

In songs, poems, and storybooks, we often like to use words that rhyme. Rhyming words have similar sounds at the end! "Cat" rhymes with "hat" because they end on similar sounds.

The words "cat" and "bat" also rhyme! Notice that these words end with the same letters. Not all rhyming words end with the same letters, and not all words that end with the same letters rhyme.

Below, there is a list of words, some of which rhyme with the one on the left. Color in all the words in a row that rhyme with the first word.

cat	**hat**	**rat**	**pan**
make	**cake**	**leak**	**bake**
same	**lays**	**name**	**aim**
boy	**lake**	**toy**	**plane**
jump	**lump**	**bump**	**slump**
red	**said**	**bed**	**point**

Match The Rhymes

Name each picture and connect the rhyming words by sound.

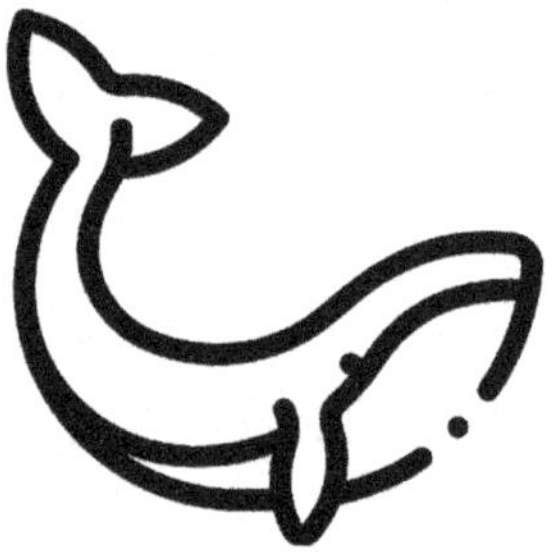

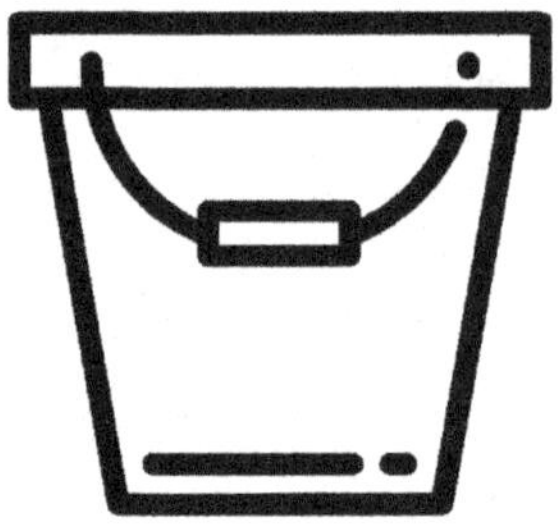

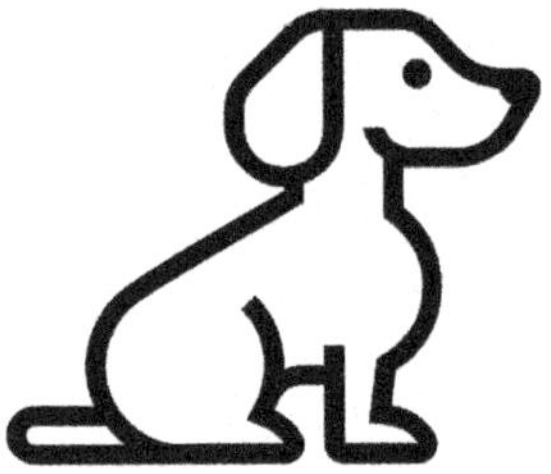

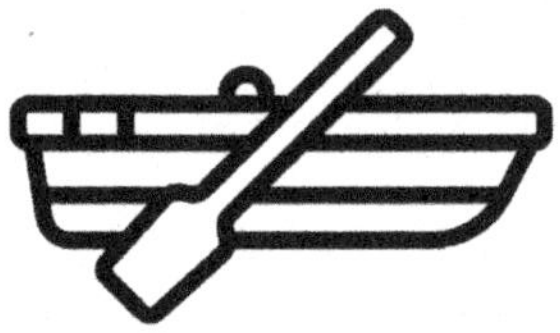

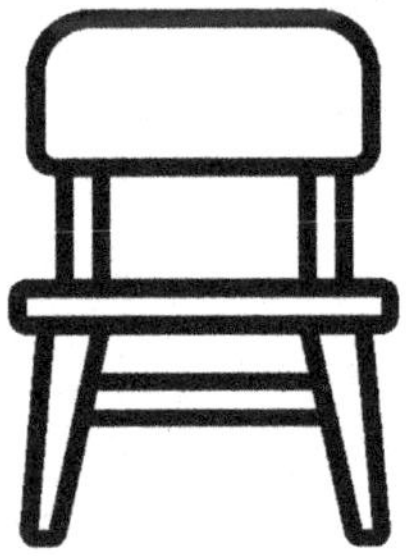

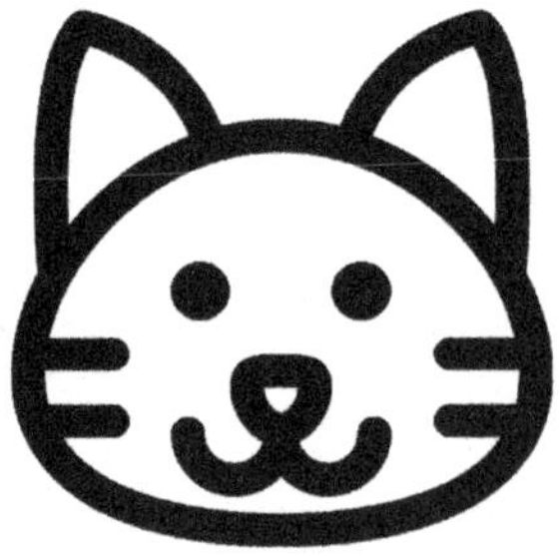

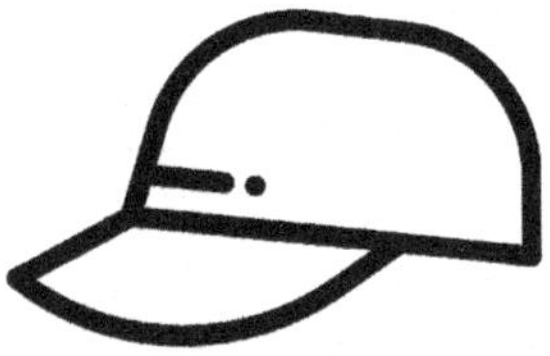

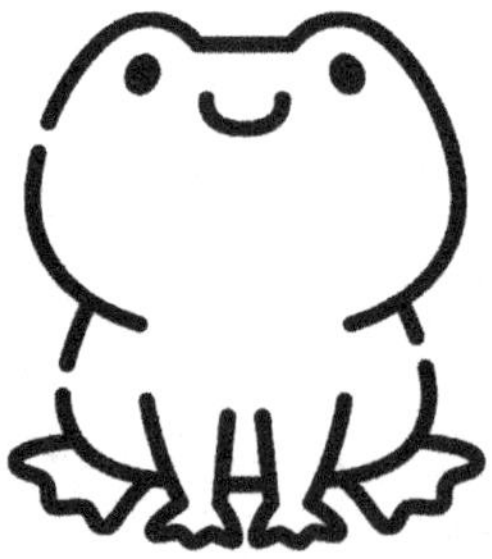

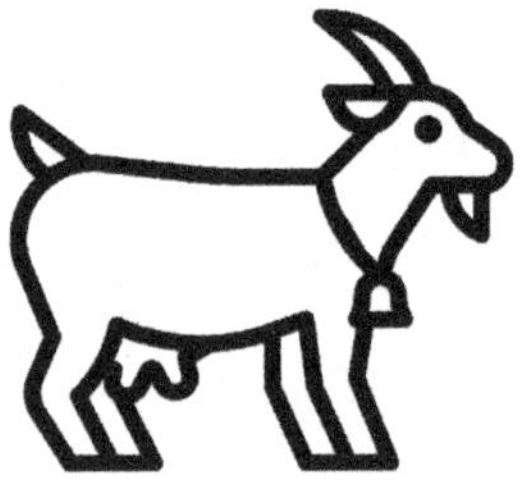

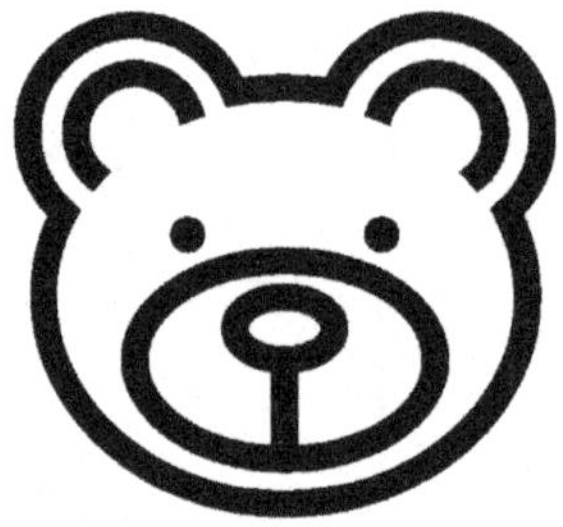

Read The Rhymes

Connect the rhyming words by spelling.

hare

slip

snake

mare

lazy

hazy

trip

rake

Strange Rhymes

Not all rhymes are spelled the same way! Read each word and note its spelling, but match the rhymes by sound again.

sigh

lane

late

fly

breeze

bait

train

please

A71

Rhyming Choice

For each word, choose the word that rhymes.

funny	**money or breeze**
better	**ease or letter**
snow	**bow or sled**
spouse	**mouse or wife**
skirt	**dirt or plane**
power	**piece or flower**

Name The Rhymes

Write rhyming labels under these pictures!

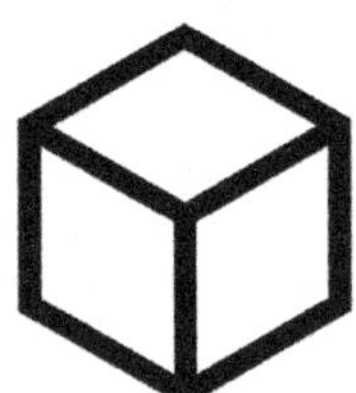

Guess The Rhyming Words

Use the clues to guess the pair of rhyming words.

I found a [smelly, black and white animal] in the [back of the car].

skunk , trunk

There is a [small animal that squeaks] in the [place where I live].

__________ , __________

I took my [pet that barks and wags its tail] and my [green pet that jumps and croaks] to play on a [tree trunk].

__________ , __________

I saw a [person who tells jokes] at the circus, and they turned my [sad or angry face] into a smile!

__________ , __________

A74

Rhyming Brainstorm

Think of a rhyme for each word.

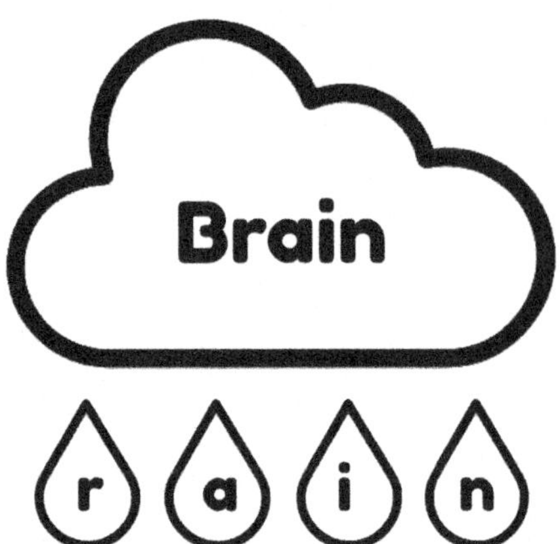

A75

Let's Write A Poem!

Fill in the blanks with rhyming words to compose a poem.

My name is Lance,
And I like to dance!
Sometimes I sweep,
Other times I sleep.
That's me, it's true,
Now who are you?

My name is ____________,
And I like ____________!
Sometimes I ____________,
Other times I ____________.
That's me, it's true,
Nice to meet you!

A76

The Six Syllable Types

A syllable is one part of a word that can be said with no breaks. It has to contain at least one vowel sound or vowel team. If you hum or clap a word, you should be able to count the syllables. Like "octopus!" If you hum octopus, it will sound something like hm-hm-hm. That's three syllables, and each one in oc-to-pus includes a vowel. Break the example words into syllables and underline the ones we're looking for.

1. Closed syllables end with a consonant, which has a short vowel before it. The whole word "cat" is a closed syllable. In octopus, "oc" and "pus" are closed syllables.

oc/to/pus   red   care/ful

2. Open syllables end with a long vowel. The whole word "cry" is an open syllable. In octopus, "to" is an open syllable.

me   octopus   baby

3. Vowel-consonant-e syllables include a magic e at the end! They end with a long vowel, a consonant, and a magic e (which is silent, but makes the earlier vowel long). The word "cake" is a VCE syllable.

snake   ride   dislike

4. R-controlled syllables include a bossy r! They have a vowel followed by the letter r, which gives the vowel a special sound.

order   thunder   stir

5. Diphthong syllables include a diphthong, or a vowel team that is said together. The word "grow" is a diphthong syllable.

cloud   flower   author

6. Consonant-le syllables end with silent es, and they have no other vowel sounds. The second syllable in "purple," pur-ple, is like this. If you say it out loud, it sounds like /pl/. They are hard to learn!

A77

Consonant -le Words

Consonant-le words have an unstressed final syllable with a consonant and the letter group -le at the end. The e is silent, and there are no other vowels in that final syllable.

Write in the c+le syllable for each word and connect it to the right picture.

purple

bubble

circle

jungle

trample

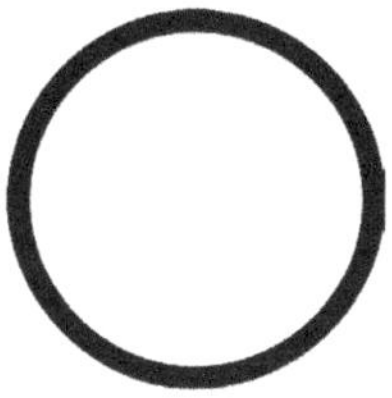

handle

A78

Sounding Out Long Words

Long words contain many different letter combinations. Try to sound out each of these long words and connect it to the right picture.

giraffe

refrigerator

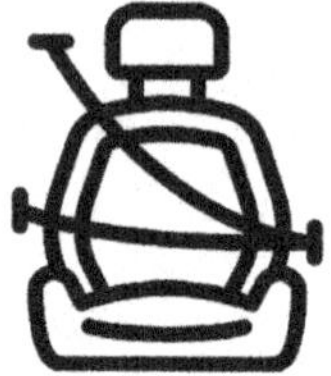

sleepover

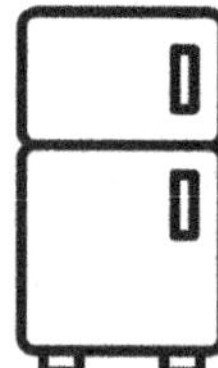

seatbelt

underwater

pillowcase

A79 Spelling Rules Are Hard To Make

There are lots of rules in English, but there are also lots of exceptions to those rules! Let's look at one rule with so many exceptions that we don't often teach it anymore.

i before e. This rule states that when the letters i and e appear together, i should come first. This is true of words like "niece" and "brief" and "relief."

Except after c! This rule states that e goes before i if they come after a c, like in the words "ceiling" and "conceit."

Now let's look at the exceptions!

In many words, e comes before i, even without a c. This is true of "weird" and "species" and "veil" and "being."

After c, i still often comes before e in words like "glacier" and "conscience" and "ancient."

Here is the start of something the Merriam-Webster dictionary tried to make up to account for every exception—as you can see, it's hard:

"I before e, except after c
Or when sounded as 'a' as in 'neighbor' and 'weigh'
Unless the 'c' is part of a 'sh' sound as in 'glacier'
Or it appears in comparatives and superlatives like 'fancier'
And also except when the vowels are sounded as 'e' as in 'seize'
Or 'i' as in 'height' [...]"

Can you think of more words that break the "i before e" rule?

A80 What's Your Name?

You've learned so many letters and sounds! Let's apply them to your name. When you're done, decorate your name tag!

How do you spell your name?

Write out all the vowels in your name:

Write out all the consonants:

How many syllables are in it? Separate them out.

Does it include blends, digraphs, diphthongs, or other letter clusters? A silent e? A syllable type you recognize? Look over the name and identify as many parts as you can!

Let's color!

In the following pages you will be able to color all the letters in the abecedary!

Aa

Acorn

Bb
Bear

Cc
Car

Dd
Duck

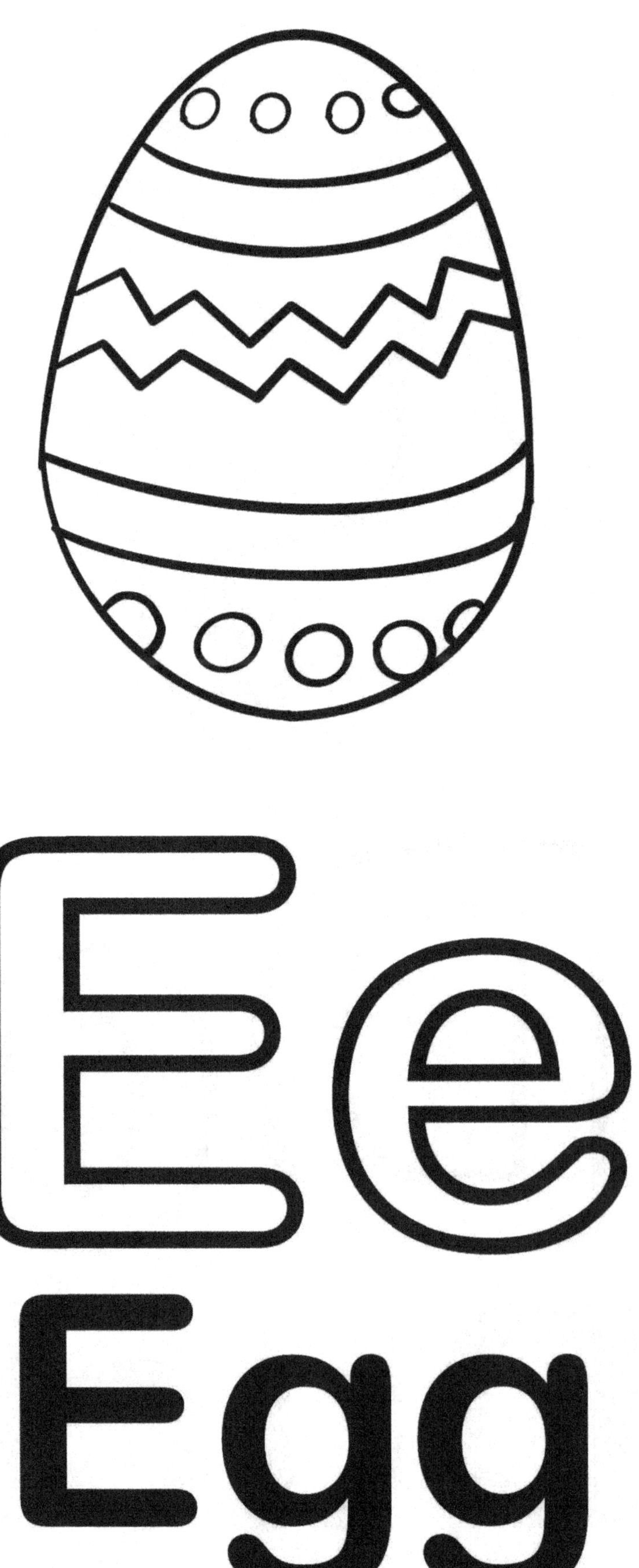
Ee
Egg

Ff
Firetruck

Gg
Goat

Hh
Hippo

Ii
Igloo

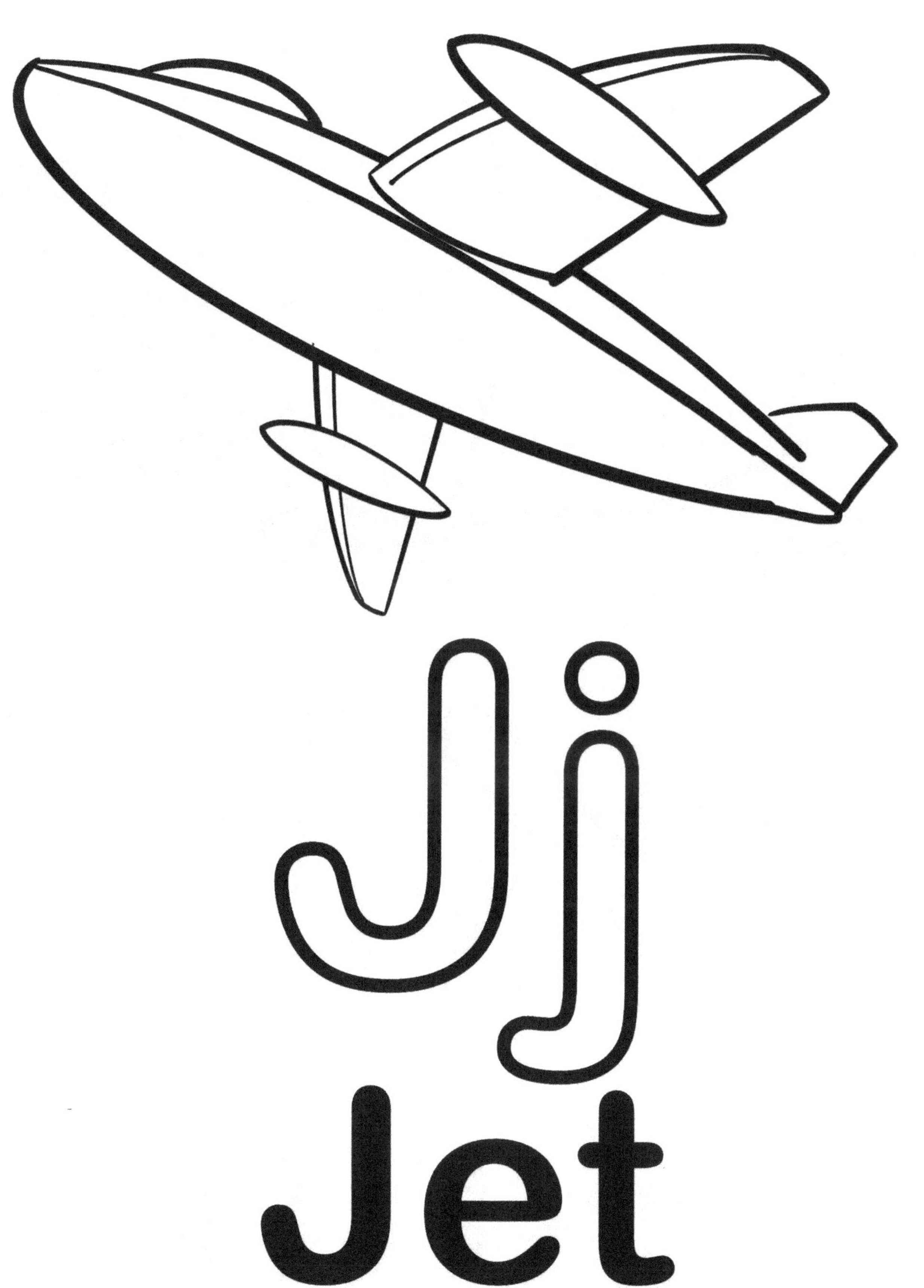

Jet

Kk
Kite

Ll
Lion

Mm
Mouse

Nn

Net

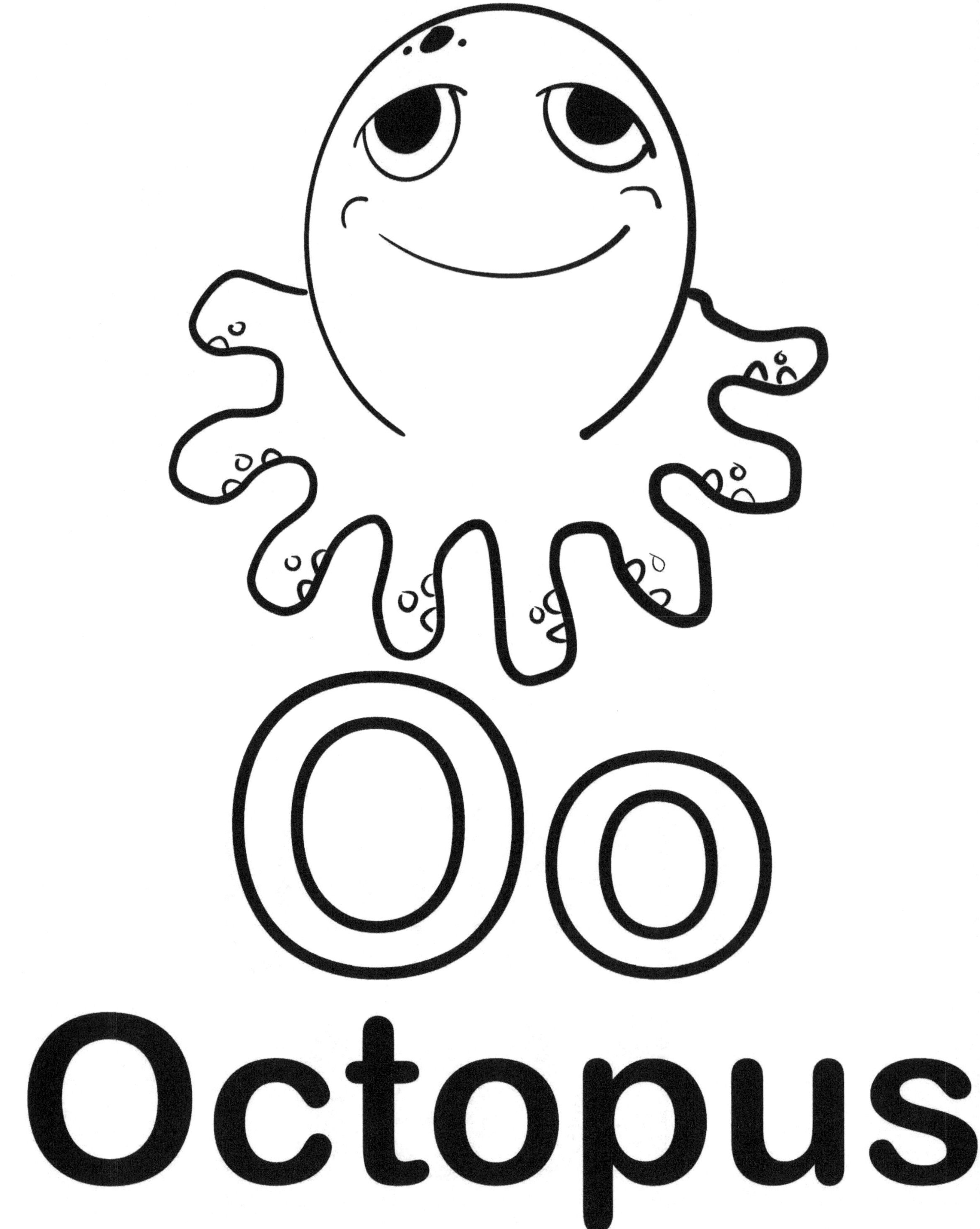
Oo
Octopus

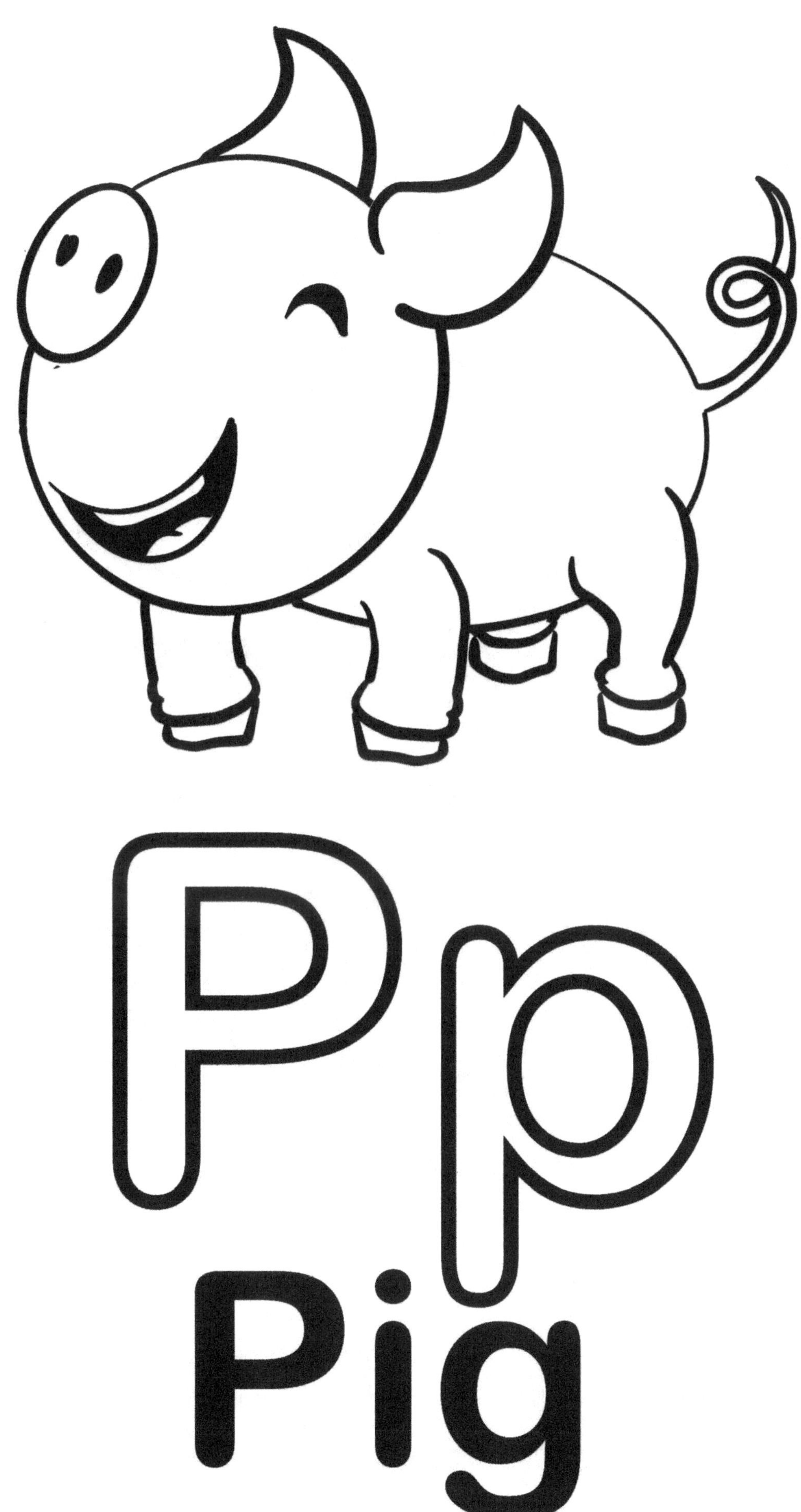
Pp
Pig

Qq
Quail

Rr
Racoon

Ss
Seal

Tt
Train

Uu
Umbrella

Vv
Vase

Ww
Whale

Xx
X-ray

Y y
Yak

Zz
Zebra

Activities Answer key

A1.-

A2.-

A3. plan, run, east, bat, hop, long, see, mom

A4. spill, carry, fuss, comment, puff // ball, dress, silly, mitt, fluffy, summer

A5. Cat, Dog, Pig, Green, Farm, Feet

A6. Bus, Ham, Fox, Jam, Pail

A7. Gift, Bird, Boat, Flag, Girl

A8. Tree, Flower, Moose, Umbrella, Octopus, Rainbow, Watermelon

Hard C	Soft C
cane	icy
cash	mice
fact	cent

A9. cat, hard; face, soft; pencil, soft

Answer key

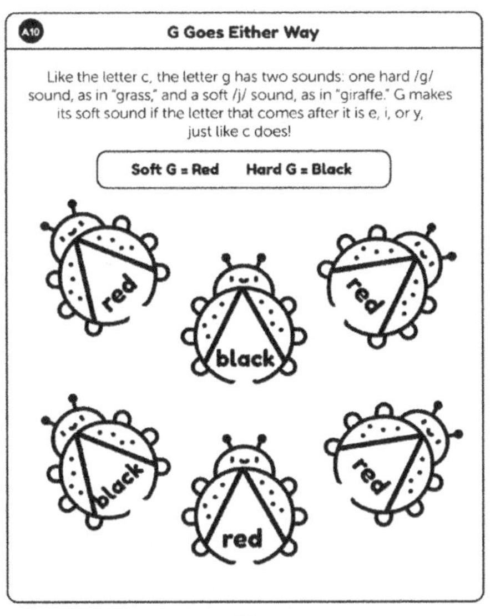
A10 G Goes Either Way

Like the letter c, the letter g has two sounds: one hard /g/ sound, as in "grass," and a soft /j/ sound, as in "giraffe." G makes its soft sound if the letter that comes after it is e, i, or y, just like c does!

Soft G = Red Hard G = Black

red

black

red

black

red

red

12

A10.

A11. -

A12. lawyer - consonant, yellow - consonant, bicycle - vowel, happy - vowel, monkey - vowel, year - consonant

A13.

Long E Sound	Long I Sound
pretty	rely
windy	fly
candy	dry
puppy	fry
lazy	apply
kitty	cycle

A14. bath, mug, wing, fish, shell, frog, map, tulip, bugs

A15. cap, log, sun, lip, bed

Answer key

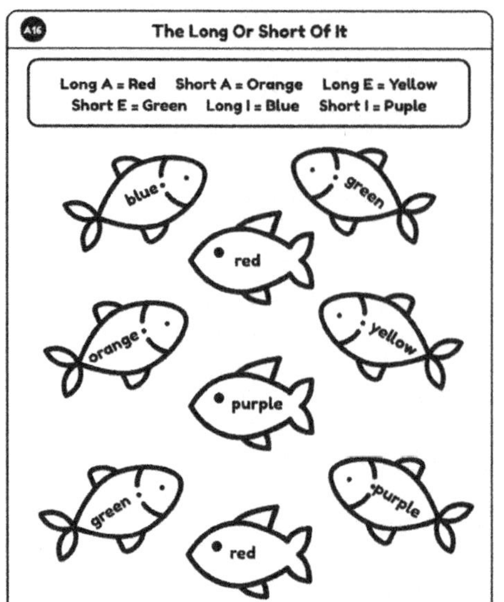

A16.

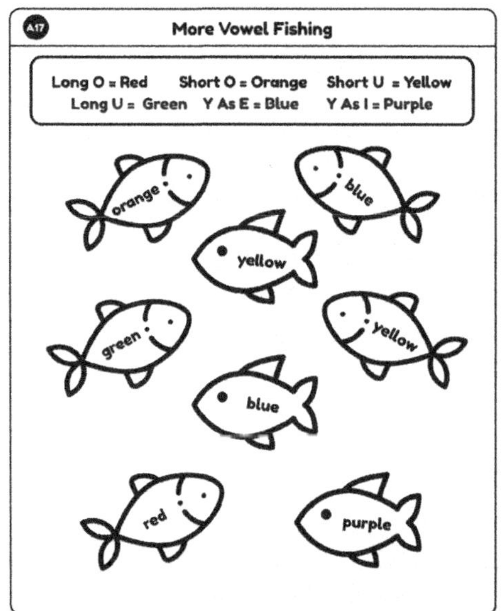

A17.

A18. Circle: ruler, purple, alarm, chair, girl, sport, car

A19. bird, yarn, storm, finger, fork, corn, chair, bear, purse

A20. hat, sun, bag // box, cup, ten, bat, win

A21. -

Answer key

A22. bath, cash, beach, pick

A23. The sun is bright when it is high in the sky. I put my clothes back in the bureau and my food back in the fridge. Today we match, and we look beautiful.

A24. sheep, cheese, cherry, shark // chalk, shell, chair, ships

A25.

Hard th sound	Soft th sound
they	bath
father	math
this	thorn
there	birthday

A26. My birthday is in a month! I am going to be eight. There will be chocolate ice cream with cherries.

A27. Blue, Wish, Bright, Catch

A28. Today I wore a scarf and a shirt with stripes. I love frogs, but not snakes. I like to play! I slide, climb trees, and splash around.

A29. -

A30. brag - blend, chips - digraph, scrape - blend, shave - digraph, grip - blend, thump - digraph, slide - blend, drove - blend, when - digraph, phone - digraph, twig - blend, plate - blend

A31. fling, dragon, price, slime, travel

A32. skunk, wasp, slab, sheep, ugly, fruit

Answer key

A33. glove, sled, clam, table, brain, agree, flower, snail, twinkle

A34. -

A35. -

A36. I have a toy owl. I will boil some stew for dinner. The noise of the fountain is soothing. I enjoy bowling! My mother taught me how to play.

A37. room, hawk, sour, grow

A38. cow, around, flower, swoop, crawl

A39. paw, toys, soup, foot // joy, noise, chew, draw

A40. -

A41.

blue	green	green	blue
purple	red	purple	red
blue	blue	blue	green
blue	purple	purple	red
purple	red	red	blue
green	green	blue	purple

free response

A42. happy, stick, equality

A43. precooked, prejudged, triangle, nonfiction, overeat

A44. unusual, impossible, injustice, nonsense, misunderstand, unhappy, mistake, nonfiction, informal // un, im, in, non, mis

Answer key

A45. replay, redo, research, retie, retell

A46. slow, brave, size

A47. boxes, coldest, pointed, fearless, meaningful

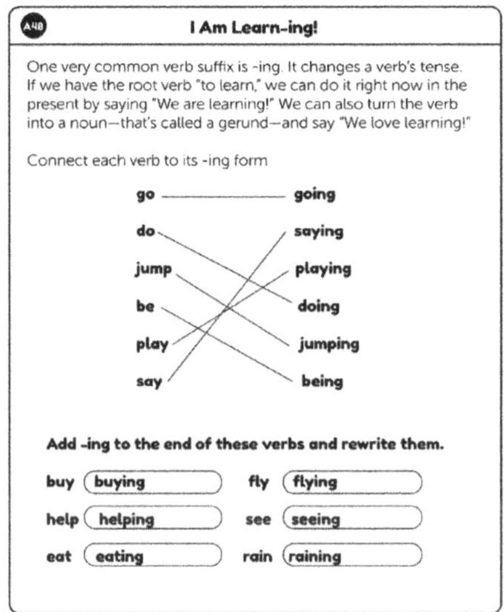

A48 **I Am Learn-ing!**

One very common verb suffix is -ing. It changes a verb's tense. If we have the root verb "to learn," we can do it right now in the present by saying "We are learning!" We can also turn the verb into a noun—that's called a gerund—and say "We love learning!"

Connect each verb to its -ing form

go	going
do	saying
jump	playing
be	doing
play	jumping
say	being

Add -ing to the end of these verbs and rewrite them.

buy	buying	fly	flying
help	helping	see	seeing
eat	eating	rain	raining

50

A48.

A49.

A Person Who	More
driver	weirder
rider	tastier
writer	easier
player	flashier
sleeper	happier

A50. cuter 2. smartest 3. nice 4. taller

A51. lawyer - suffix, predestine - prefix, trees - suffix, nicest - suffix, singer - suffix, untold - prefix, lightest - suffix, untrue - prefix

Answer key

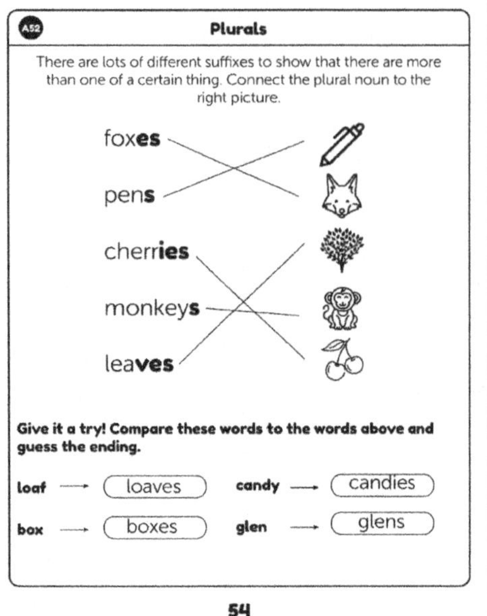
A52 **Plurals**

There are lots of different suffixes to show that there are more than one of a certain thing. Connect the plural noun to the right picture.

fox**es**
pen**s**
cherr**ies**
monkey**s**
lea**ves**

Give it a try! Compare these words to the words above and guess the ending.

loaf → loaves
candy → candies
box → boxes
glen → glens

54

A52.

A53. uni- 1, bi- 2, sept- 7, oct- 8, pent- 5, tri- 3, quar- 4, quin- 5

A54.I am reading a nonfiction book about bicycles! Prehistoric dinosaurs are the coolest; I am learning about them in school. The flowering trees in these photos I am reviewing are beautiful! I am happiest out in nature. I am unhappy because I dislike being graded down for misspelling words.

A55. mane, tube, cape, kite

A56. cake, bat, map, take, mare

A57. bug - no, cut - yes - cute, div - yes - dive, cat - no, ros - yes - rose, pan - no, leg - no

A58. cute, nice, nose, face, love

A59. rat, slid, fin // bee, toe, doe

Answer key

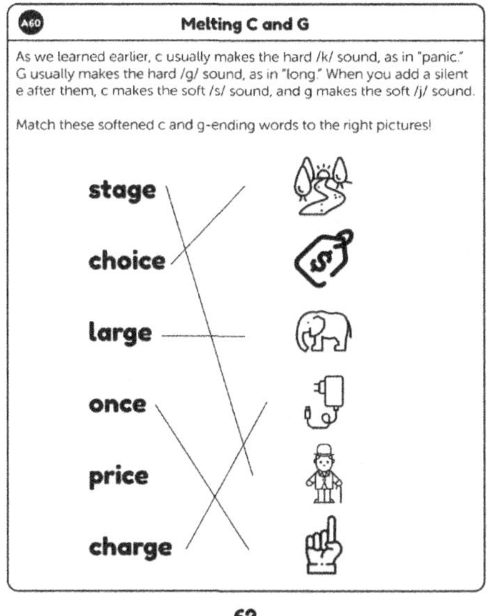

A60 **Melting C and G**

As we learned earlier, c usually makes the hard /k/ sound, as in "panic." G usually makes the hard /g/ sound, as in "long." When you add a silent e after them, c makes the soft /s/ sound, and g makes the soft /j/ sound.

Match these softened c and g-ending words to the right pictures!

stage
choice
large
once
price
charge

62

A60.

A61. b i b, s oo t, p r y, ch i p, k i t, s a t, th u mb, p i t, b e d, l i mb, r o p

A62. plate, oval, shine, taste, lace, bake, awake, wave

A63. rake, tape, plane, robe, snake, lake, pine, dine, cake

A64. write sign honor crumb knight // The wreath on my door has bright red berries. I know that Mary had a little lamb. The watch on my wrist says it will be eight in an hour.

A65 **Silent Letter Match**

Match the words with silent letters to their pictures! Circle or underline the silent letter in each word.

crumb
sword
ghost
scissors
knot
sign

67

A65.

Answer key

A66. climb, wrist, knob, science, wrap

A67. make - bake, cake; same - name, aim; boy - toy; jump - lump, bump, slump; red - said, bed

A68.

A69.

Answer key

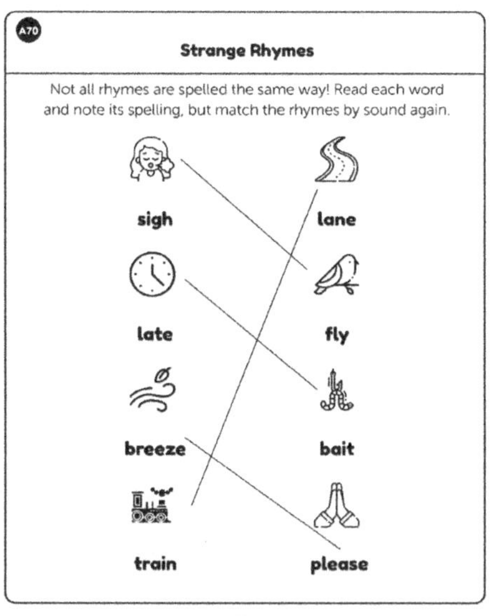

A70.

A71. funny - money, better - letter, snow - bow, spouse - mouse, skirt-dirt, power - flower

A72. block - clock, sail - pail, map - cap, king - ring

A73. mouse, house; dog, frog, log; clown, frown

A74. Free answer

A75. Free answer

A76. me, oc/to/pus, ba/by; snake, ride, dis/like; or/der, thun/der, stir; cloud, flow/er, au/thor

Answer key

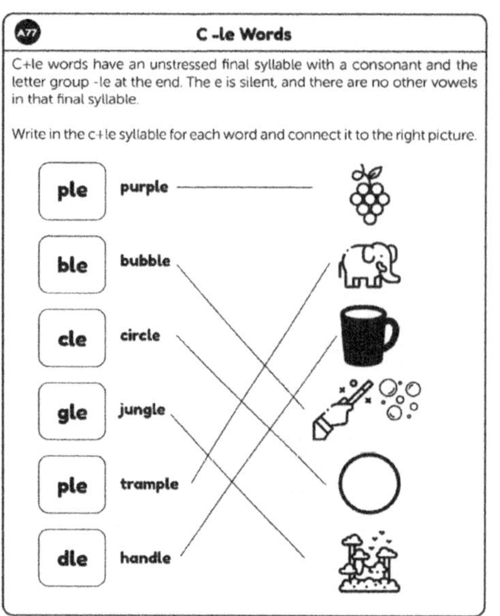

C -le Words

C+le words have an unstressed final syllable with a consonant and the letter group -le at the end. The e is silent, and there are no other vowels in that final syllable.

Write in the c+le syllable for each word and connect it to the right picture.

ple purple

ble bubble

cle circle

gle jungle

ple trample

dle handle

79

A77.

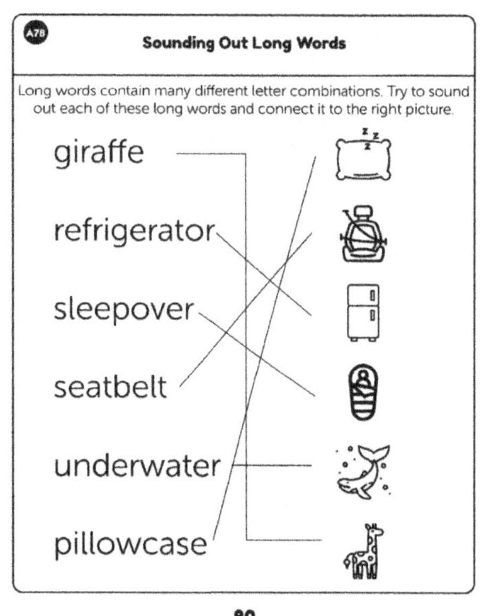

Sounding Out Long Words

Long words contain many different letter combinations. Try to sound out each of these long words and connect it to the right picture.

giraffe

refrigerator

sleepover

seatbelt

underwater

pillowcase

80

A78.

A79. Free response

A80. Free response

CONGRATULATIONS!

Excellent work! I am sure that there were some obstacles along the way, but you persisted and finished the activities! Hooray!

I also want to give a HUGE THANKS to our staff at Kids Castle Press for making these books a reality. It wouldn't have been possible without them. Feel free to visit our website below to show them some love!

In addition, if you'd like us to send you more free content to print out, you can do so by visiting our website: www.kidscastlepress.com

Lastly, if you like this book, would you be so kind as to drop me a review on Amazon? To add a cherry on top... You can email us for a chance to win a free physical copy of our next book: info@kidscastlepress.com

Don't miss out as we won't be doing this forever... it's a limited time only!

Thank you very much!

Jennifer L. Trace

PHONICS PRO CERTIFICATE

____

Date: ____________ **Signed:** ____________

Made in United States
Orlando, FL
14 June 2023